D0049110

MANAGEMENT MESS

TO

LEADERSHIP SUCCESS

MANAGEMENT MESS

TO
LEADERSHIP
SUCCESS

30 Challenges to Become the
Leader You Would Follow

SCOTT JEFFREY MILLER

Executive Vice President, FranklinCovey

Mango Publishing

CORAL GABLES

Published by Mango Publishing Group, a division of Mango Media Inc.

Cover & Layout Design: FranklinCovey Creative Lab and Jermaine Lau

For permission requests, please contact the publisher at:

Franklin Covey Co.
2200 W. Parkway Blvd.
Salt Lake City, UT 84119 USA
Attention: annie.oswald@franklincovey.com

For special orders, quantity sales, course adoptions, and corporate sales, please email the publisher at sales@mango.bz. For trade and wholesale sales, please contact Ingram Publisher Services at customer.service@ingramcontent.com or +1.800.509.4887.

Management Mess to Leadership Success: 30 Challenges to Become the Leader You Woud Follow

Library of Congress Cataloging
ISBN:(p) 978-1-64250-088-2 (e) 978-1-64250-089-9

Library of Congress Control Number: 2019938550

BISAC category code: BUS071000 BUSINESS & ECONOMICS / Leadership, BUS041000 BUSINESS & ECONOMICS / Management, BUS019000 BUSINESS & ECONOMICS / Decision-Making & Problem Solving

Printed in the United States of America

TABLE OF CONTENTS

PART 3

GET RESULTS

A FINAL THOUGHT

WHAT ABOUT CHARACTER?

INTRODUCTION

I'm proud of you. You're bold—courageous, even. You're holding a book with the words "Management Mess" prominently featured on the cover. Never mind that people nearby—perhaps on a train or plane, standing in line at Starbucks, or your colleagues around the office—could see you holding this book and immediately associate you with the word "mess." You could have easily been showing off a different book with a different title: *The Burden of Perfection; The Genius's Guide to Leadership;* perhaps even *From Great to Greater.* People would definitely be impressed seeing you read a book like that. But that's not me, and I suspect that's not you either. I didn't attend an Ivy League school, and I don't peruse the heady academic tomes on the latest management theories. I came up through the leadership trenches. I had no idea what I was doing, but I had enough ambition and drive to keep at it, even when I failed—and I failed often.

I wrote this book for those who feel they weren't perfectly groomed for leadership—those with a bit of a "mess" in them, whether that comes from being an outsider, a lack of experience, a lack of training, or all of the above. There are likely people I know who think I'm the *last* person who should write a book like this, probably a few people reading it right now. So I'll get this next part out of the way:

I have an intense personality that's often turned up to 11. I've been mean, petty, selfish, and self-absorbed. I've made genuinely good people cry, no doubt caused talented associates to choose to leave the organization and, regrettably, used my position and temper to sometimes belittle, demean, and stifle the contributions of others. But I'm also known as the leader whose division you join if you want your career and skills to blossom. I'm a close friend to many, and I'm the guy you call at any hour to bail you out of jail, a bind, or any other emergency. I'm also the guy who keeps a chilled bottle of champagne ready to pour for impromptu houseguests. I am an honorable husband and a nurturing father; a champion, supporter, and mentor to countless people who have experienced extraordinary success in their careers. I have a handful of God-given abilities I work hard to use and magnify (humility is not one of them). I am, in short, a human being: I have flaws and talents; failures and triumphs.

If you're a fellow traveler along the leadership path, I've written this book for you. It's a reflection of my experiences, both messes and successes, run through the crucible of the real world—shaped, validated, and often corrected by the deep expertise and thought leadership of many colleagues, friends, and mentors at FranklinCovey. I was lucky to have landed at FranklinCovey—a company that provides industrial-strength management and leadership advice to the Fortune 5000 and beyond, throughout the world. So, even as I careened and sometimes crashed through the ranks, I couldn't help but pick up on the principles and practices that the most successful leaders get right. These proven insights (many of which are included in this book) helped an admittedly imperfect leader rise to the C-suite.

I'll be one of the first to admit leadership isn't always rewarding. It can feel like a bottomless pit of problem solving and adult-sitting. Leadership is exhausting, repetitive, and requires a constant stretch of your emotional and intellectual skills. It demands an "always on" mentality, as you're expected to have all the right answers and make all the right decisions, often on the fly. Most days, candidly, I really don't enjoy it. But it doesn't mean leadership isn't important; on the contrary, often the things we struggle with yield the biggest return (nobody drinks a kale smoothie because it tastes good). It's okay if you admit that leadership can be hard and unenjoyable. We're travelers on this road together. But the benefits of being successful at it can be life-changing.

Maybe you're ambitious and bright, but leadership hasn't exactly felt like a calling from on high. Perhaps you're the first person in your family to attend college, let alone a board meeting. Or maybe you skipped college altogether. Maybe you're a woman rising to the top of a male-dominated industry or a veteran starting to make their way through the business world and drawing from a very different set of leadership styles and experiences. Maybe you're the person asked to lead the same people who, days earlier, were your peers, or perhaps you're the highly regarded MBA who has to lead someone like *me*. If so, this book is for you and anyone else who approaches leadership with a sense of unease, trepidation, or feeling like an outsider.

Of course, no single person is a complete "management mess," nor has anyone I've known been a total "leadership success." We are a bundle of varying talents and fears, expressed through the daily decisions we make. I wrote this book to broaden those talents, set aside limiting fears, and promote better leadership decisions. To accomplish this, you'll find 30 challenges, honed by FranklinCovey through years of research and development, tens of thousands of client implementations, and countless coaching engagements. I've referenced the various thought leaders and experts behind these challenges throughout, representing a collection of wisdom, expertise, and practical advice spanning more than four decades. I've also highlighted individuals who have impacted me as exemplars of a particular principle, and shared stories of people who fell into a management mess—altering names and identities, unless I'm referencing myself (which my wife believes is way too often for a book of this size).

The challenges in this book will make you a better leader and are organized into three parts: "Lead Yourself" (Challenges 1–8), "Lead Others" (Challenges 9–21), and "Get Results" (Challenges 22–30). If you're not put off by examining how principles can collide with the real world, or how I've had to learn many leadership lessons the hard way, I invite you to take each of them to heart. You can read them from 1 to 30, or skip to topics that resonate the most in the moment. At the end of each challenge, you'll find prompts for moving from "mess to success." How you choose to implement these is up to you—pick one a day if you're feeling up to it, or one a week. Whatever the cadence, do your best to take the challenges off the pages of the book and into your real-world leadership roles.

So let your colleagues see you reading a book with "Management Mess" on the cover. Break it open at lunch and proudly sit across from your boss! Because inside, the principles and practices collected here come from some of the best leadership minds around. Use my experiences with them as a shortcut, a cautionary tale, or a skill worth adopting. I promise you, I won't be pulling any punches. And since you're only thirty practices away from having more successes (and fewer messes) in this adventure we call leadership, let's get to it.

PART 1

LEAD YOURSELF

Day 1	Day 2	Day 3	Day 4	Day 5
Demonstrate Humility	Think Abundantly	Listen First	Declare Your Intent	Make and Keep Commitments
Day 6	Day 7	Day 8	Day 9	Day 10
Carry Your Own Weather	Inspire Trust	Model Work/Life Balance	Place the Right People in the Right Roles	Make Time for Relationships
Day 11	Day 12	Day 13	Day 14	Day 15
Check Your Paradigms	Lead Difficult Conversations	Talk Straight	Balance Courage and Consideration	Show Loyalty
Day 16	Day 17	Day 18	Day 19	Day 20
Make It Safe to Tell the Truth	Right Wrongs	Coach Continuously	Protect Your Team Against Urgencies	Hold Regular 1-on-1s
Day 21	Day 22	Day 23	Day 24	Day 25
Allow Others to Be Smart	Create Vision	Identify the Wildly Important Goals® (WIGs®)	Align Actions with the Wildly Important Goals	Ensure Your Systems Support Your Mission
Day 26	Day 27	Day 28	Day 29	Day 30
Deliver Results	Celebrate Wins	Make High-Value Decisions	Lead Through Change	Get Better

CHALLENGE 1

DEMONSTRATE HUMILITY

Has your lack of humility ever limited your perspective or lessened your influence as a leader? Would you even know if it had?

It was an important two days in my early leadership career. After a successful four years as an independent salesperson, I had been recently promoted to lead a group of about ten peers. Most of them had preceded me on the team, invested in and developed their own sales skills, and in some ways were more talented than I was as a consultative sales representative.

I'd shown some leadership promise as the new leader and wanted to start it off memorably. (Stay tuned for that part, I promise not to disappoint in this opening challenge.) After securing the vice president's approval and funding, I planned a two-day sales-strategy meeting. I organized the conference room, secured the catering, and hired one of our internal performance consultants to facilitate a two-day training to ensure this team was up to date on our latest leadership solution.

The first morning arrived, and the consultant, Nancy Moore, and I both showed up around 7 a.m. for the 8 o'clock announced start. I remember it well. I was excited and likely amped after one too many cups of coffee. (In fact, one *was* too many in Provo, Utah.) Nancy was also very invested in the trainees' success and even brought a platter of beautifully arranged and freshly cut fruit for them (something she assembled herself, not one of those displays you buy ready-made from the grocery store). I was ready for my leadership debut. This was going to be epic. Team members began to stroll in around 8:15. We finally started around 8:30 when the last associate showed up.

I was incensed. I managed to open the meeting, introduced the consultant, and took my place at the U-shaped table. But I was consumed by the fact that on my first day as their leader, my team would disrespect both the consultant and me by being so cavalier with the start time. After all, we're experts at time management; how could they all show up late and not even apologize? It stewed in me, and like most issues that irritate me, it metastasized and took on a life of its own.

I went through the day fixated on the profound disrespect. The team knew I was annoyed because I made zero attempt to conceal it. The concept of self-regulation and managing my emotions was not even in my lexicon at the time.

It continued to agitate me into the evening and the next morning. On the way to the office, I stopped at the grocery store, not to buy fruit or croissants, but to buy ten copies of the *Salt Lake Tribune*. I had a plan, and it was going to be legendary. Leadership in action, people.

I entered the room at exactly 8:00 a.m., our starting time. To my sadistic delight, few were in their seats. Ten or so minutes passed before everyone was finally seated. I stood up, in what I thought would be one of my finest leadership moments, and began to walk around the table. I pulled the classified ads out and tossed them in front of each person, announcing, "If you want a job from nine to five, Dillard's is hiring." And in case they didn't get the point, I passed out yellow markers so they could highlight any openings.

This was what being a successful leader was all about! I was making an important point and would be respected for my candor, boldness, and strength.

At least, it seemed like a great idea at the time.

LET'S JUST SAY I WASN'T BORN WITH THE HUMILITY GENE. I STRUGGLED WITH IT AS A FIRST-TIME MANAGER, AND I STRUGGLE WITH IT NOW. I HAVE TO REALLY WORK AT REMEMBERING ITS VALUE IN MY RELATIONSHIPS, ESPECIALLY AS A LEADER.

Rather than acknowledging my leadership genius, people began getting up from their tables and leaving. Many shot me looks that ranged from confusion to sheer repugnance. Still others began telling me off, more than one threatening to quit on the spot. I did what any good leader would do under such circumstances: I doubled down. This was on them after all, not me.

Maybe not the best strategy. Nancy stood frozen, watching in disbelief. One colleague announced it was his last day. There was a general theme to the arguments against me: How could the team leader, the same one sponsoring a leadership-training session, so blatantly disregard the leadership principles being taught?

Calling that moment a leadership mess is probably kind. Because this was nearly twenty years ago, how we all managed to take a collective breath and salvage the moment is a bit fuzzy. I am sure it had more to do with them than me, but we somehow reassembled about an hour later and finished the day.

If you think I had a leadership *mea culpa* that morning, you'd be wrong. For days I privately insisted to Nancy that I was in the right. To her credit, she patiently listened to my absurd rationalization. A week or so later, she finally sat me down and helped me understand why my technique had not served me well. It was hard for me to see her point, but I trusted her to have my best interests in mind, and so took the lesson to heart. I did my best to make it up to the team and apologize for my actions.

You might be surprised to learn I'm friends with every person who was in the training room that day. Many of them came to my wedding a decade

WHEN YOU LEARN TO EMBRACE HUMILITY, YOU FEEL MORE COMFORTABLE BECAUSE YOU KNOW WHO YOU ARE. YOU CAN LET GO OF THE FEAR OF MAKING MISTAKES OR THE NEED TO NEVER SHOW WEAKNESS. TO QUOTE OUR COFOUNDER DR. STEPHEN R. COVEY, "HUMBLE LEADERS ARE MORE CONCERNED WITH WHAT IS RIGHT THAN BEING RIGHT."

later, and we laughed and cried at the absurdity of it all. In fact, several of them re-created the scene at my reception in front of my new wife of only 120 minutes. I'm sure she must have been worried that she'd just committed to a sociopath. In the end, we all marveled at my profound ignorance and arrogance.

Or said another way, my total lack of humility.

Let's just say I wasn't born with the humility gene. I struggled with it as a first-time manager, and I struggle with it now. I have to really work at remembering its value in my relationships, especially as a leader.

In my role as executive vice president for thought leadership at FranklinCovey, I am privileged to host several interview programs, both on the Internet and iHeartRadio. After interviewing more than a hundred bestselling authors, CEOs, and leadership experts, the one commonality they all share when defining a great leader is humility. They see humility as a strength, not a weakness. You might argue that the opposite of humility is arrogance.

Leaders who fail to demonstrate humility often find themselves leaning toward arrogance and seeking outside validation. They rarely listen to anyone but themselves, and thus miss opportunities to learn and course-correct. They often turn conversations into a competition and feel the need to "one-up" others and have the final say.

In FranklinCovey's bestselling book *Get Better: 15 Proven Practices to Building Effective Relationships at Work*, Todd Davis writes:

"Those who are humble have a secure sense of self—their validation doesn't come from something external, but is based on their true nature. To be humble means to shed one's ego, because the authentic self is much greater than looking good, needing to have all the answers, or being recognized by one's peers. As a result, those who have cultivated humility as an attribute have far greater energy to devote to others. They go from being consumed with themselves (an inner focus) to looking for ways to contribute and help others (an outer focus). Humility is the key to building solid character and strong, meaningful connections."

When you learn to embrace humility, you feel more comfortable because you know who you are. You can let go of the fear of making mistakes or the need to never show weakness. To quote our cofounder Dr. Stephen R. Covey, "Humble leaders are more concerned with what is right than being right."

FROM MESS TO SUCCESS:
DEMONSTRATE HUMILITY

- Pick an initiative you're leading or participating in.

- Identify someone whose perspective on the initiative is different from yours.

- Schedule time to listen to their perspective. When they differ substantially, exercise the patience and respect to not just understand, but to genuinely consider their point of view.

- What did you learn that might measurably improve the initiative? the relationship? your own leadership style?

- Become more comfortable, even confident, in not having all the answers yourself. This a strength, not a weakness.

Day 1	Day 2	Day 3	Day 4	Day 5
Demonstrate Humility	Think Abundantly	Listen First	Declare Your Intent	Make and Keep Commitments
Day 6	Day 7	Day 8	Day 9	Day 10
Carry Your Own Weather	Inspire Trust	Model Work/Life Balance	Place the Right People in the Right Roles	Make Time for Relationships
Day 11	Day 12	Day 13	Day 14	Day 15
Check Your Paradigms	Lead Difficult Conversations	Talk Straight	Balance Courage and Consideration	Show Loyalty
Day 16	Day 17	Day 18	Day 19	Day 20
Make It Safe to Tell the Truth	Right Wrongs	Coach Continuously	Protect Your Team Against Urgencies	Hold Regular 1-on-1s
Day 21	Day 22	Day 23	Day 24	Day 25
Allow Others to Be Smart	Create Vision	Identify the Wildly Important Goals® (WIGs®)	Align Actions with the Wildly Important Goals	Ensure Your Systems Support Your Mission
Day 26	Day 27	Day 28	Day 29	Day 30
Deliver Results	Celebrate Wins	Make High-Value Decisions	Lead Through Change	Get Better

CHALLENGE 2

THINK ABUNDANTLY

Where is scarcity in your thinking impeding the best results? How difficult is it for you to share credit, praise, recognition, or power?

You've probably had occasion to dine at a buffet (except for my sophisticated wife, who abhors them). There are two schools of thought when approaching the line: first, there's only a finite amount of food, so grab everything you want before someone else does. On the other hand, you might believe that there's plenty of food to go around, more than anyone could possibly finish, so you can let the elderly man with the oxygen tank go ahead. There will be, in fact, enough shrimp for everyone. Remember, they arrived frozen in a 40-pound bag, after all.

It's essentially the difference between a *Scarcity Mentality* (get yours before it's gone) and an *Abundance Mentality* (there's plenty to go around for everyone).

My first lesson in the power of thinking abundantly came from a colleague. I was deciding whether to move from Provo, Utah, to the ski town of Park City, about 50 miles away. Same job, just a longer commute, living in a cooler town (about as different as skim milk is from tequila). The relocation would almost double my rent, and I was trying to determine if this was a good financial decision (to be clear, it wasn't). As I was talking with this work friend, he said something I will never forget: "You'll never have enough until you define how much is enough." I've shared that aphorism with countless friends, because it speaks to the heart of abundance thinking. Define "enough," or you'll be constantly worried you don't have it.

> THINKING ABUNDANTLY IS ESSENTIALLY THE DIFFERENCE BETWEEN A SCARCITY MENTALITY (GET YOURS BEFORE IT'S GONE) AND AN ABUNDANCE MENTALITY (THERE'S PLENTY TO GO AROUND FOR EVERYONE).

My second lesson was a little more brutal and, appropriately enough for our culinary metaphor, happened over lunch. (I have a proven method for choosing restaurants for business meetings. If I expect the exchange to be high-stakes, I like being in a secluded booth on neutral ground. I never have difficult conversations in my favorite restaurants, so I can distance the emotion of the meeting from my affinity for the food.)

On this occasion, I had scheduled lunch at one of my favorite restaurants, Cracker Barrel, because I was expecting a pleasant meal with one of my most trusted team members, Jimmy. Imagine my surprise when he ordered his country-fried steak and said, "Scott, I'm tired of you taking credit for all of my projects."

That sentence needs no translation. Further context? Yes, please.

Jimmy continued by sharing specific instances where he felt I had overshadowed his work: announcing the results of a campaign he'd led, talking up a product launch he'd planned, etc. In each case, I had never even mentioned his contribution.

My first instinct was to disagree, and with a healthy dose of indignation. The old me certainly would have done that—I used to pride myself on telling people the way things were, damn the consequences. But working at FranklinCovey had changed me, and I inhaled a measured breath between the stimulus of the moment and my chosen response. I did my best to validate Jimmy's concern and commit to being more aware of the issue.

After lunch, I began to unpack what he'd said. How much of it was true? Certainly, I had no reason to hoard credit. At that point in my career, my influence in the firm was substantial and my track record with the CEO and the board was exceptional. Was I so insecure that I needed *more* attention and accolades than I already had? Was reaching up for that next rung on the career ladder more important than helping someone else up? Had I really, consciously or subconsciously, managed my brand, reputation, and career at his expense?

I believe the executive team would tell you that, in their presence, I frequently lift others up and acknowledge their contributions. But what happens in a closed-door session with management doesn't always get passed on to other employees. So, what went wrong this time?

I had failed to think abundantly.

It's human nature to feel scarcity when we fear we won't have enough—money, gifts, attention, praise, fill in the blank. Was there really a finite amount of credit in the firm? Clearly, no. To use the buffet metaphor, I kept ladling "credit" on my plate like a pile of shrimp. Not only had I not stopped to consider "what was enough," I was driven by a scarcity mindset that made me fearful of missing out. Worst of all, I wasn't even *aware* that I thought that way.

After my conversation with Jimmy, I made a conscious effort to publicly praise anyone who truly warranted it, and share credit when my team had shone independent of me. I haven't always been

> I MADE A CONSCIOUS EFFORT TO PUBLICLY PRAISE ANYONE WHO TRULY WARRANTED IT, AND SHARE CREDIT WHEN MY TEAM HAD SHONE INDEPENDENT OF ME. I HAVEN'T ALWAYS BEEN PERFECT BUT BY REMEMBERING THE PRINCIPLE OF ABUNDANCE, I BELIEVE I'VE BECOME A MORE GRACIOUS, GENEROUS, AND RESPECTFUL LEADER. AND NOT ONLY DO I NOT MISS OUT, I'VE FOUND MORE REWARD IN THE ACCOMPLISHMENTS OF OTHERS.

perfect since then, but by remembering the principle of abundance, I believe I've become a more gracious, generous, and respectful leader. And not only do I not miss out, I've found more reward in the accomplishments of others.

FROM MESS TO SUCCESS:
THINK ABUNDANTLY

- Think of a situation where you can share credit, praise, and recognition, or decision-making power.

- When you catch yourself believing you alone should be recognized for success or achievement, pause and reflect deeply: Why? What is the cause? "Peel the onion" around your scarcity thinking.

- Reflect on your unforgettable (good or bad) career moments. Is there a pattern?

- List how you could think and act more abundantly going forward.

- Address other areas of your life where scarcity thinking could be limiting you and your ability to lift others up. Envision the impact of having an Abundance Mentality throughout your life.

Day 1	Day 2	Day 3	Day 4	Day 5
Demonstrate Humility	Think Abundantly	Listen First	Declare Your Intent	Make and Keep Commitments
Day 6	**Day 7**	**Day 8**	**Day 9**	**Day 10**
Carry Your Own Weather	Inspire Trust	Model Work/Life Balance	Place the Right People in the Right Roles	Make Time for Relationships
Day 11	**Day 12**	**Day 13**	**Day 14**	**Day 15**
Check Your Paradigms	Lead Difficult Conversations	Talk Straight	Balance Courage and Consideration	Show Loyalty
Day 16	**Day 17**	**Day 18**	**Day 19**	**Day 20**
Make It Safe to Tell the Truth	Right Wrongs	Coach Continuously	Protect Your Team Against Urgencies	Hold Regular 1-on-1s
Day 21	**Day 22**	**Day 23**	**Day 24**	**Day 25**
Allow Others to Be Smart	Create Vision	Identify the Wildly Important Goals® (WIGs®)	Align Actions with the Wildly Important Goals	Ensure Your Systems Support Your Mission
Day 26	**Day 27**	**Day 28**	**Day 29**	**Day 30**
Deliver Results	Celebrate Wins	Make High-Value Decisions	Lead Through Change	Get Better

CHALLENGE 3

LISTEN FIRST

When was the last time you listened to
understand rather than to reply?

I have a propensity to interrupt. I'm not proud of this, but I'm also not usually aware I'm even doing it. Maybe it's in my DNA and I missed my calling in life to be a courtroom litigator or CIA interviewer. Either way, if you've seen me in action at a dinner party, you've likely witnessed this behavior on display.

Most of my conversations follow the same self-defeating cycle: To show genuine interest in the other person, I ask questions. Repeatedly. In rapid-fire succession (like a boxing kangaroo deploying the full speed and power of its feet against its victim). Rarely do I give the other person time to answer before I'm on to the next query. Embarrassingly, I know this because my wife will often put a hand on my arm and say, "Scott, let them finish."

Why would I do this? It might be to circumvent my social awkwardness. In fact, because of a compulsion to fill any silent space, I frequently ask the same question over an hour or two, to the point where people must think I'm suffering from early dementia, which is no joking matter. My attempt to develop rapport and fill the silence usually creates more awkwardness and lessens my credibility. It also puts people on the defensive—maybe a great asset if you're an attorney cross-examining a witness, but in all my roles, not so much.

It's easy to see how interrupting works against listening. When others are talking, we're in our own mind formulating a response, crafting a rebuttal, or outright abandoning any mental engagement because we vehemently disagree with such an absurd position. *How could you possibly think that?* is something I think (or worse, say) way too often. But I'm working on it.

I've recently become the host of a new radio program called *Great Life, Great Career.* In this setting, I've discovered not only the importance of silence, but its necessity. As I interview many talented thought leaders and industry giants, I've found that it's important for people to have space to consider the question I've asked—to be allowed time to put a mental peg in their thoughts and hang more meaning there. And neuroscience backs up everything I'm learning on the job.

Several years ago, I met one of my heroes, Deborah Tannen, the famed Georgetown University professor of linguistics and bestselling author. Her seminal book *You Just Don't Understand* claimed the #1 *New York Times* bestseller position for an amazing eight consecutive months.

During our conversation, she taught me a listening skill I need to use more often. She pointed out that when two speakers have a different sense of how much pause is normal between turns, the one who expects shorter pauses can get the impression that the shorter-pauser is finished when they're not, or has nothing to say when they do. The result can be an unintended interruption. If you find yourself doing all the talking, she suggests you count to 7—or, if necessary, 10—before you begin speaking, to give the other person more time to continue or begin speaking. You might be amazed that they do have something to say. On the other hand, if you feel interrupted, or feel like the other person is hogging the floor, you can push yourself to begin speaking sooner than what feels natural to you, and may be amazed to see that the other person will stop and actually listen.

Here's my take on this: When someone else is talking, purposely close your mouth and focus on the physical sensation of your lips being pressed together (your own lips, not yours to theirs). And when the other person has paused, count to 7 before responding. Doing so will increase the likelihood that they'll continue, often sharing crucial details about their point of view or situation. I'm convinced that one of the first steps to becoming a better listener, in addition to actually changing your mindset or beliefs (Challenge 11) about the value of listening, is to simply stop talking. Eliminating—or even just lessening—your own interruptions through a small measure of heightened awareness can pay profound dividends in your relationships.

It turns out we don't invest a lot of time in listening. I often poll leaders in my keynote speeches around the world and ask how many have had formal training around their communication skills. About 70 percent of the audience raise their hand. Then I further define communication to include business writing, media training, public speaking, facilitation skills, and the use of presentation software. At that point, nearly 100 percent have their hand raised. I then pause and ask another question: "How many of you have had formal training or education on effective *listening*?" I can easily count the number, even in a large audience of five hundred or more attendees.

Listening is one of the most undervalued communication skills, and it's rarely taught to leaders. Instead, we're instructed to clarify our messages, communicate with confidence and persuasion, and master the words we use. At most, we get lip service paid to the value of just shutting up and listening. We lead meetings, town halls, conference calls, webcasts,

IT'S EASY TO SEE HOW INTERRUPTING WORKS AGAINST LISTENING. WHEN OTHERS ARE TALKING WE'RE IN OUR OWN MIND FORMULATING A RESPONSE, CRAFTING A REBUTTAL, OR OUTRIGHT ABANDONING ANY MENTAL ENGAGEMENT BECAUSE WE VEHEMENTLY DISAGREE WITH SUCH AN ABSURD POSITION. HOW COULD YOU POSSIBLY THINK THAT? IS SOMETHING I THINK (OR WORSE, SAY) WAY TOO OFTEN. BUT I'M WORKING ON IT.

retreats, and offsites—the list is endless. We're busy convincing, coaching, clarifying, then starting over and doing it again. Those are hard things to do silently via pantomime or gesticulation. When was the last time you voted for a candidate, followed a leader, or donated money to someone because you liked how they listened or gestured? Too often in a world where people are clamoring to be heard, we view listening as irrelevant or weak. Telling—now that's a strength. Whether delivered through TED, by pundits over news channels, or by high-priced keynote speakers, there's an entire telling industry out there waiting to be heard (and paid).

So why the bias toward telling? Here's my succinct answer: Listening sucks. It often requires a generous gift of time and attention to forget about your own needs and focus intently on someone else's. To really listen requires discipline, self-control, and a genuine desire to understand the other person's point of view. Listening requires you to care, perhaps even more than you may want.

And the skill of listening isn't simply a nice trait for leaders to have—it's a true leadership competency. Dr. Covey, in his renowned book *The 7 Habits of Highly Effective People*, inspires us to become more empathic listeners. Empathic Listening means we listen first, with an open, respectful mindset of *Let me try to understand this person's needs, goals, pressures, and feelings*. It's very selfless: you consciously rid yourself of any distractions and focus intently on what the other person is saying. As a result, you can accurately repeat the content of what they said and the person's intent to their own satisfaction—not only the words, but the feelings and emotions behind the words.

Dr. Covey also expands on four specific types of poor listening techniques we commonly default to:

- Evaluating (agree or disagree using our own experience as reference)

- Probing (ask questions using our own experience as reference)

- Advising (give counsel using our own experience as reference)

- Interpreting (make assumptions about the other person's motives using our own experience as reference)

I'll illustrate these poor listening techniques via a sample conversation that Judy Henrichs, an executive coach and leadership consultant, recently shared with me. Assume someone walks into your office and announces, "*My dog just died.*" Here's what the poor listening techniques might sound like:

The Evaluating Listener:

"You shouldn't feel bad; it's just a dog, after all. I know someone who lost their parents when they were only six years old and then you won't believe what happened next..."

This may seem extreme, but it's not really that far-fetched. We make constant judgements about people based on our own needs, paradigms, and beliefs. We may try to help, but we do the opposite—we are focused on our own agenda and timeline.

The Probing Listener:

"Was it her heart? Cancer? Hit by a car?"

This may seem well-intended, but again, it's a reflection of your *own* agenda. The facts and details are more important to you than the grieving pet owner. It's also a bit macabre. Why do you need to know *how* someone's dog died? Does it really matter? Unless they tell you, it's immaterial. Probing is focused on satiating your own needs for details that create meaning for you or allow you to respond.

The Advising Listener:

"Whatever you do, don't have them cremated. I once heard a story about how the..."

By advising, you've arrogantly determined what the other person's problem is. You've decided their challenge is how to properly dispose of their dog's body. You've not taken any interest or time to understand what it is they may (or may not) be struggling with.

The Interpreting Listener:

"Well, you wouldn't be so sad if you hadn't invested so much in that damn dog. I mean, good grief, how much have you spent on those ridiculous massages? And that pet psychic? She was a total kook."

First, are you sure sadness is their primary emotion? It might be relief, or even guilt. Or loneliness. Likely, this person is or was sad, but that's not for you to be guessing at. Whatever experiences are coloring the interpreting listener's point of view (perhaps their own pet psychic revealed their hamster is entertaining murderous thoughts) has no bearing on what the other person is going through.

These four responses may seem exaggerated, but we've all probably been guilty of them. Empathic listeners engage not just their ears, but their eyes, mind, and heart to truly understand what's going on. They face the other person, not turning away or looking over their shoulder. They look for visible signs to help tell the full story, such as the person looking worn out or slumped over. They don't focus on their own frame of reference or agenda. It's not effortless—it takes investment and interest to listen empathically. It also takes practice and selflessness.

Practically, being a great listener will increase your ability to effectively partner with others to solve the right problems in the right way. So the next time you ask a question that on the surface seems to show a genuine interest, ask yourself: *What's my motive? What do I truly need to know to demonstrate empathy? Am I on my agenda and timeline, or theirs?*

It can actually be freeing to put yourself aside and focus on someone else for a bit. Allow yourself to get out of your own head and internal narrative and just put your attention on the other person. Leave yourself open and allow them to just be. Spending time in that quiet place of connection with someone else in their angst, their joy, or their frustration can create bonds that will last a lifetime, and also can keep your own struggles in context.

FROM MESS TO SUCCESS:
LISTEN FIRST

- Practice not interrupting by gently putting your lips together and counting to 5 after the other person appears to have finished speaking. The more you practice this technique, the more natural it will become.

- Demonstrate Empathic Listening by striving to understand the other person's needs, goals, pressures, and feelings. Recognize when you are on your agenda versus theirs.

- When you find yourself interrupting, giving advice, agreeing or disagreeing, probing, or telling your own story... stop. Check back in and listen intently to understand what the other person is saying and how they're feeling.

- If the other person specifically asks for your suggestions or feedback, you may provide it.

- Recognize the value of time as a gift—you can't meet the needs of everyone, but you can do your best to meet the needs of the person in front of you.

Day 1	Day 2	Day 3	Day 4	Day 5
Demonstrate Humility	Think Abundantly	Listen First	Declare Your Intent	Make and Keep Commitments
Day 6	**Day 7**	**Day 8**	**Day 9**	**Day 10**
Carry Your Own Weather	Inspire Trust	Model Work/Life Balance	Place the Right People in the Right Roles	Make Time for Relationships
Day 11	**Day 12**	**Day 13**	**Day 14**	**Day 15**
Check Your Paradigms	Lead Difficult Conversations	Talk Straight	Balance Courage and Consideration	Show Loyalty
Day 16	**Day 17**	**Day 18**	**Day 19**	**Day 20**
Make It Safe to Tell the Truth	Right Wrongs	Coach Continuously	Protect Your Team Against Urgencies	Hold Regular 1-on-1s
Day 21	**Day 22**	**Day 23**	**Day 24**	**Day 25**
Allow Others to Be Smart	Create Vision	Identify the Wildly Important Goals® (WIGs®)	Align Actions with the Wildly Important Goals	Ensure Your Systems Support Your Mission
Day 26	**Day 27**	**Day 28**	**Day 29**	**Day 30**
Deliver Results	Celebrate Wins	Make High-Value Decisions	Lead Through Change	Get Better

CHALLENGE 4

DECLARE
YOUR INTENT

Have you ever had incorrect intent ascribed
to your actions? Why did that happen?

If you'd asked me about declaring my intent during my early, rough-and-tumble, push-my-way-to-the-top leadership years, I would have told you that you were nuts. If you think of leadership as a war of political gamesmanship and cutthroat advancement, then you'll likely resonate with this Victorian military advice: *"Conceal your purpose and hide your progress; do not disclose the extent of your designs until they cannot be opposed, until the combat is over."*

IN THE CORPORATE WORLD, DUE IN NO SMALL PART TO THE WORK OF FRANKLINCOVEY AND SOME OF OUR WELL-RESPECTED COMPETITORS, MACHIAVELLIAN ATTITUDES HAVE EVOLVED INTO THE DESIRE TO BUILD CULTURES OF HIGH TRANSPARENCY, COLLABORATION, AND TRUST. TODAY, FEW PEOPLE WANT TO WORK IN ENVIRONMENTS OF CONCEALMENT AND ONE-UPMANSHIP.

This adversarial mindset used to be commonplace in almost every organization—part of an "eat or be eaten" culture. It may still be the prevailing wisdom while driving in New York City (where signaling your intention to change lanes only invites other drivers to mash the accelerator and close the space), but that's another story. In the corporate world, due in no small part to the work of FranklinCovey and some of our well-respected competitors, Machiavellian attitudes have evolved into the desire to build cultures of high transparency, collaboration, and trust. Today few people want to work in environments of concealment and one-upmanship.

If this outdated belief describes your leadership style and work culture, let me save you some time and heartache. In the long run, you will lose—and lose badly. Once you gain the reputation for deception and concealing your true intentions, no one (and I mean no one) will trust you. And without trust, you're doomed.

Just ask the trust expert, Stephen M. R. Covey. In his bestselling book *The Speed of Trust*, he writes, "We judge ourselves by our intentions and others by their observable behavior." So even if you actively try to conceal what you're up to, people will judge you based on what they see. If you want to succeed, don't withhold information—openly share. State your intent so others can't misinterpret your actions.

I'll never forget a principle I was taught in a public relations class. Loosely interpreted, it was, "Absent real facts, people make stuff up." Declaring our intent in conversations, especially in adversarial or high-stakes conversations, is crucial to creating mutual understanding, if not mutual agreement.

A few months ago, "Peter," a junior colleague, scheduled a meeting with me in Outlook. Although there wasn't an agenda, or even a subject line, I agreed to meet out of respect for him. I didn't know this person very well, so a meeting was unusual but not out of line. As a result, we sat somewhat uncomfortably in a conference room where the conversation, primarily led by Peter, meandered for about fifteen minutes. It touched on a variety of loosely linked topics with questions, comments, and even judgments on nearly every project I was leading. Peter seemed to want to give me feedback, but because the topics were so far-ranging and scattered, I couldn't discern what to focus on.

> DECLARING OUR INTENT IN CONVERSATIONS, ESPECIALLY IN ADVERSARIAL OR HIGH-STAKES CONVERSATIONS, IS CRUCIAL TO CREATING MUTUAL UNDERSTANDING, IF NOT MUTUAL AGREEMENT.

Finally, as I was losing my patience, I asked matter-of-factly about the purpose of the meeting. Peter stammered and attempted to clarify, but continued to meander for a few more increasingly irritating minutes. Eventually, I said, "I'm sorry, I'm still not clear on the purpose of our conversation. We're touching on a broad range of topics, but I don't understand how I can help you." Let me add that I think Peter is a fine person, high in character, hardworking, well educated, and dedicated. We might not see all things eye to eye, but he reminds me of a younger version of myself (that's both a compliment and a critique). However, because I was listening with increasing suspicion, I wondered if this was worth my time. Truly, people matter—but so did the two major projects I needed to land that day.

I labored once again to gain clarification. This time, Peter declared what had been on his mind all along. It was a topic completely different from any of the "ground softeners" up to that point. Peter had a very clear point of view on something that needed my support. He now spoke with convincing language, and I leaned in and listened intently. That's one benefit of declaring your intent—as human beings, thoughts and emotions are swirling around inside our head as someone is talking. In fact, we spend much of our attention and energy discerning people's intent and working through how we'll respond. But declaring one's intent cuts through much of the noise and mental static that impedes true listening. And that's what I found had happened to me. Suddenly, all the irritation and negative stories percolating in my head vanished and I could focus on the real issue. Unfortunately, it had taken nearly fifty-five minutes of a sixty-minute meeting to get there!

After the meeting was over and we were walking out of the conference room, Peter said to me, "That went better than I thought."

I replied, "What do you mean?"

"You're quite intimidating, Scott," he continued, "and I thought this would be a very difficult conversation."

Wow! I had been frustrated, even angry, at Peter's lack of organization and clarity. Turns out that his inability to talk straight and declare up front his intent was partially based in fear. I'm guessing he'd been clear on his intent in his mind, but my previous behaviors and reputation had likely led him to believe my "brand" was one of arrogance and intimidation. Now, let's be clear, I'm not taking responsibility for his share of the meeting. I'm just more mindful now of how I can contribute positively or negatively to others living this principle.

The next time you're in a conversation where something could be left open to misinterpretation, remember this thought from Dr. Blaine Lee, author of *The Power Principle: Influence With Honor:* "Nearly all, if not all, conflict arises from mismatched or unfulfilled expectations." Make sure that what you intend people to hear and see is what they actually hear and see. The less clear you are, the more you are responsible for their lack of clarity.

FROM MESS TO SUCCESS:
DECLARE YOUR INTENT

- Take stock of how often you begin conversations by declaring your intent—are you clear about your goals, or are you leaving people to guess?

- Early on, ask others to confirm they are clear on your intent.

- Consider how you make it safe (or unsafe) for others to declare their intent. What should you stop doing, do more of, or do differently?

- Think of a cordial relationship where you have mutual respect but suspect the other person has read you wrong or doesn't fully understand where you're coming from. Try meeting them informally (like for coffee), and see if you can work a declaration of intent into the conversation.

- Ensure when you declare your intent that it's truthful and congruent with your actions.

- Expressing your intent may well take a level of courage that might not be natural to you. Better to summon that skill than face the consequences that follow from not doing so.

Day 1	Day 2	Day 3	Day 4	Day 5
Demonstrate Humility	Think Abundantly	Listen First	Declare Your Intent	Make and Keep Commitments
Day 6	Day 7	Day 8	Day 9	Day 10
Carry Your Own Weather	Inspire Trust	Model Work/Life Balance	Place the Right People in the Right Roles	Make Time for Relationships
Day 11	Day 12	Day 13	Day 14	Day 15
Check Your Paradigms	Lead Difficult Conversations	Talk Straight	Balance Courage and Consideration	Show Loyalty
Day 16	Day 17	Day 18	Day 19	Day 20
Make It Safe to Tell the Truth	Right Wrongs	Coach Continuously	Protect Your Team Against Urgencies	Hold Regular 1-on-1s
Day 21	Day 22	Day 23	Day 24	Day 25
Allow Others to Be Smart	Create Vision	Identify the Wildly Important Goals® (WIGs®)	Align Actions with the Wildly Important Goals	Ensure Your Systems Support Your Mission
Day 26	Day 27	Day 28	Day 29	Day 30
Deliver Results	Celebrate Wins	Make High-Value Decisions	Lead Through Change	Get Better

CHALLENGE 5

MAKE AND KEEP COMMITMENTS

Are you damaging your credibility through
too many unfulfilled commitments?
Are you a serial overcommitter?

It turns out, making commitments is easy for me. At the time of this writing, I've committed to:

- Host a weekly radio program on the topic of leadership on iHeartRadio.

- Simultaneously author or coauthor three books.

- Write a weekly blog post.

- Author a weekly column in *Inc.* magazine.

- Host a weekly Web interview program.

- Tape a daily leadership insight for radio and social media.

- Teach a class at my church.

- Lead a fundraising initiative.

- Serve on a marketing committee.

- Provide career coaching to four or five people at any given time.

- Get to the gym and work out.

- Raise three boys.

- Stay married, given all the above.

And a bevy of other, no less significant items. Your list will be unique to your role and life, but I bet it comes in at a similar length.

The problem in this challenge is about making and *keeping* commitments. Now I have to deliver on everything—and so do you! And here's my candid admission: I will drop the ball on at least one of these. I'm perpetually overcommitted and can't possibly deliver on everything at the level of excellence I want. How about you?

Many of the challenges in this book reflect the tension between what I *thought* an effective leader was early in my career, and what the reality turned out to be. And for some reason, this particular challenge is one I keep having to relive because I'm not quite figuring it out. To quote a colleague of mine, "I fully understand the principle; I just have yet to adopt it into my life."

Given the caliber of advice I've been getting over the years, you'd think I'd have this challenge figured out. Even back in 2007, when I was assuming a new role at FranklinCovey, a peer told me: "Scott, underpromise and overdeliver."

And like most prescient counsel, her words haunt me to this day.

At the time, I discounted what this colleague had told me because I thought it betrayed something other than a "do whatever it takes" work ethic. (In retrospect, it didn't.) But I remember the spirit of her counsel: *Don't take on too much, Scott, and perpetuate your brand of delivering on some projects and not on others. Simply do what you say you're going to do and do it with extraordinary impact.*

I'M PERPETUALLY OVERCOMMITTED AND CAN'T POSSIBLY DELIVER ON EVERYTHING AT THE LEVEL OF EXCELLENCE I WANT. HOW ABOUT YOU?

I have a habit of ascribing too much value to activity and not enough to discerning what should be done with the highest quality. Not that my work is sloppy—on the contrary, I would maintain that my deliverables are exceptional. *But only the ones I actually deliver on.* And now even that might be at risk. My career portfolio has its share of projects I committed to (that most people forgot about, I hope) that never reached liftoff. I actually don't have a problem saying no. I say no all day long. But I love yes more, particularly with projects that allow me to think big in terms of vision, impact, and uniqueness. Plus, the little voice in the back of my head argues that even if I disappoint 15 percent of the people by not delivering, the remaining 85 percent will think I'm a rock star.

Contrast this with Stephen M. R. Covey, one of the leading global authorities on trust. Stephen is in demand: his famed book *The Speed of Trust* has sold over two million copies. While he's keynoting multiple times weekly and it's not unusual for him to be in four countries in four days, he's also very cautious about making commitments. Unlike me, he means everything he says. When he says no, he means it. And when he says yes, he means it. He starts and finishes. If I'm 8 for 10, Stephen's 8 for 8!

Recently I approached Stephen about increasing his global profile, and suggested we meet to brainstorm how to have him accelerate his authorship for some major business publications. He initially said, "No, thank you." With courtesy and respect, which is his style, he explained that his low profile as a columnist or contributor wasn't from a lack of opportunity—he'd been approached by numerous publications about writing columns or articles and had declined most of them. He was simply unwilling to place himself in a situation where he might disappoint someone by missing a deadline or not delivering.

If you've seen Stephen speak at a conference or your own company event, you know one of his hallmarks, beyond his indisputable credibility, is his thoughtful preparation. He is maniacal about researching a client and customizing his content to their cultural and market issues, and listening to their needs to ensure his time with them is impactful. In fact, he declines nearly as many speaking opportunities as he accepts, as further engagements might reduce his prep time for those already committed to. He literally leaves money on the table daily to ensure those he's already agreed to work with receive his best. It's rare to see companies or individuals say no to business if it comes at the expense of delivering their best to previous commitments. How many of us have done the opposite and said yes, compromising not only our current commitments, but also the ones we just took on?

To quote Roger Merrill, Dr. Covey's coauthor on the book *First Things First*: "When you make a commitment, you build hope; when you keep it, you build trust." Everyone's bandwidth is different in terms of their capacity to take on and execute their commitments with excellence. If you find yourself in the mess of overcommitting and underdelivering, consider exercising uncharacteristic restraint the next time you're approached by a colleague, friend, or family member. They may be unwittingly attempting to move you past your breaking point. Our capacity to do is always more than our capacity to do with excellence. No reasonable person can resist a response like:

I ACTUALLY DON'T HAVE A PROBLEM SAYING NO. I SAY NO ALL DAY LONG. BUT I LOVE YES MORE, PARTICULARLY WITH PROJECTS THAT ALLOW ME TO THINK BIG IN TERMS OF VISION, IMPACT, AND UNIQUENESS.

"I truly would love to be a part of that, but I'm so cognizant of not wanting to disappoint you and others I've already committed to that I'll have to decline. If something changes with my current level of commitments, I'll surely reach out to you. Thank you so much for your trust in me."

If this is hard to do in the moment, keep in mind a shorthand version: *"Let me get back to you on that."* This simple phrase gives you space between the request and the response—time to consider your commitments and availability. If you have to come back and decline, crafting a nicely worded response can be seen as even more thoughtful than if you had dismissed the request out of hand from the beginning.

Remember that fundraising initiative I listed as one of my commitments? There's good news and bad news. The good news is, I'm finished. The bad news is, they're not!

I'll end this challenge here. I love yes. But I need to love no much more. Remember, 8 for 8 is *way* better than 8 for 10. The difference is in the second number in the ratio, not the first (and that's the whole point).

FROM MESS TO SUCCESS:
MAKE AND KEEP COMMITMENTS

- Choose a project or relationship that needs your attention.

  1. Identify an unfulfilled commitment in this area.
  2. How can you realistically follow through with it?
  3. Acknowledge to the person your awareness of having not (yet) met your commitment, and recalibrate expectations on whether and when you will.

- Exercise integrity in your next "moment of choice" by being willing to politely say no.

- Inventory your current commitments. Realistically determine whether you need to unwind some of them. Your greatest gift may be to back out before you fail them and further violate expectations.

- Make sure your commitments are balanced—work, play, health, growth, outreach, etc.

Day 1	Day 2	Day 3	Day 4	Day 5
Demonstrate Humility	Think Abundantly	Listen First	Declare Your Intent	Make and Keep Commitments
Day 6	**Day 7**	**Day 8**	**Day 9**	**Day 10**
Carry Your Own Weather	Inspire Trust	Model Work/Life Balance	Place the Right People in the Right Roles	Make Time for Relationships
Day 11	**Day 12**	**Day 13**	**Day 14**	**Day 15**
Check Your Paradigms	Lead Difficult Conversations	Talk Straight	Balance Courage and Consideration	Show Loyalty
Day 16	**Day 17**	**Day 18**	**Day 19**	**Day 20**
Make It Safe to Tell the Truth	Right Wrongs	Coach Continuously	Protect Your Team Against Urgencies	Hold Regular 1-on-1s
Day 21	**Day 22**	**Day 23**	**Day 24**	**Day 25**
Allow Others to Be Smart	Create Vision	Identify the Wildly Important Goals® (WIGs®)	Align Actions with the Wildly Important Goals	Ensure Your Systems Support Your Mission
Day 26	**Day 27**	**Day 28**	**Day 29**	**Day 30**
Deliver Results	Celebrate Wins	Make High-Value Decisions	Lead Through Change	Get Better

CHALLENGE 6

CARRY YOUR OWN WEATHER

How would your team describe your leadership style when things are stormy? when things are calm?

In the 1980s, Stone Kyambadde was a semipro soccer (known as football to the rest of the world) player on the cusp of ascending to the Ugandan National Football League. During a match, an opponent intentionally injured Stone's knee, ending his football career in a split second. Stone was forced to re-create his life, his legacy, and his future. Instead of wallowing in self-pity, Stone channeled his passion for football into coaching and developing a local team for at-risk youth in Kampala, Uganda. Through the sport, Stone mentored young men to become responsible, proactive adults in the midst of poverty and violence. Thirty years later, the team is thriving, and Stone shares his positive message of hope and endurance around the world.

Stone appears in a video highlighted in FranklinCovey's *The 7 Habits of Highly Effective People*® work session as a model of a "Transition Person"—someone instrumental in breaking cycles of negative behaviors and decisions. (Visit ManagementMess.com to view this compelling video.) Stone exemplifies many leadership traits: proactivity, choice, forgiveness, vision, compassion, and dedication, to name a few. But the one trait I believe Stone illustrates best is called "carry your own weather." This idea deals with how reactive we can be to outside influences. Leaders who carry their own weather exercise emotional discipline and resist the temptation to allow external dramas to distract them.

Who doesn't struggle with this? I certainly do. Self-regulating your emotions is a key part of your EQ (emotional maturity). As I look back at my professional career, I could sum up my progress best as "two steps forward, one step back." It's headed in the right direction, but the inputs—delivering on a business result (two steps forward)—compete against my choice of outputs: acting like a jackass later that day (one step back). My brand is high on outputs and high on offenses—never illegal, immoral, or unethical; just consistently reacting impulsively to something that, with a bit more self-control, wouldn't have damaged my credibility or modeled bad behavior for others.

WHEN WE'RE TRIGGERED EMOTIONALLY, IT'S EASY TO FORGET WE HAVE A CHOICE AS TO HOW WE WILL RESPOND. CENTRAL TO HABIT 1: BE PROACTIVE, FROM THE 7 HABITS, IS THE CONCEPT THAT BETWEEN WHAT HAPPENS TO US AND HOW WE REACT EXISTS A SPACE. IN THAT SPACE LIES OUR FREEDOM AND POWER TO CHOOSE OUR RESPONSE.

Beyond Stone, I know another person who exemplifies this concept better than anyone I've encountered. He happens to be Bob Whitman, Chairman and CEO of FranklinCovey. Now, I know what you're thinking: This is my well-placed chance to suck up to the person reviewing both this book and my compensation plan. But you'd be mistaken if you thought I could influence any issue with him by writing a glowing (kiss-up) assessment of his leadership skills. Don't I wish that were true. With a life full of tremendous success, Bob has also faced significant challenges. His ability to rise above such trials and model this principle makes his example even more noteworthy.

I have spent thousands of hours in the CEO's office. Bob always remains calm. He's anchored like nobody I've met, even when presented with information that would throw me and most others completely sideways. Carrying your own weather doesn't mean being devoid of emotion. Bob's not robotic by any measure; he gets frustrated and irritated like all of us. However, he carries his own weather by intentionally managing his temperament. He's hard to ruffle because he keeps his "emotional rudder" tightly aligned to the guiding values that make up his core belief system, and he never allows other people or situations to impact that alignment. Bob once told me that a real leader's true mettle is demonstrated by how closely aligned they are on the outside with how they think and feel on the inside. Damn that's hard! I'd say that's as close to complete authenticity as it gets.

So let's get real. Are there times when I wish Bob would celebrate more? Most definitely. Are there times when I can't believe he doesn't react more sternly to someone's outrageous behavior? Yes, just not mine, please. He remains a superb example of carrying his own weather at all times, highs and lows.

When we're triggered emotionally, it's easy to forget we have a choice as to how we will respond. Central to Habit 1: Be Proactive®, from The 7 Habits, is the concept that between what happens to us and how we react exists a space. In that space lies our freedom and power to choose our response. We all experience situations where it's tempting to react quickly and without thought. This is where the choice of carrying your own weather manifests itself.

To carry your own weather:

- Define your personal and professional values (from which your behaviors will be exhibited in both good and rough weather).

- When faced with a situation that threatens to hijack your emotions, stop. Take a breath and think carefully about the response you won't have to apologize for and that leaves people whole.

- Consciously calibrate your response to avoid a regretful revisit later. Recognize that most flash responses won't represent how you feel an hour (let alone a day) later. Consider saying: *"Could I have a few hours to think about my position so that it is congruent with what I am going to think and feel later on?"*

- Don't allow highly emotional people to suck you into their vortex. Not every conversation necessitates an immediate response from you. Sometimes a simple "Thank you for sharing" is enough.

When carrying your own weather, remember that you are your own meteorologist. If you don't like the weather, change it.

FROM MESS TO SUCCESS:
CARRY YOUR OWN WEATHER

- Identify people or circumstances that cause you to react emotionally.

- When these situations occur:

    1. Use the strategies listed on the previous page.
    2. If you need more time to react to an emotional conversation or situation, take it. Go for a walk, or do whatever activity allows you to disengage from the emotions of the moment. Stop, think, and evaluate the situation or stimulus and the response that aligns with the true you, then proceed.
    3. If drafting a difficult or an emotional email response, don't send it until you've reflected on the message at least twice. Consider sending it to yourself to reread and rewrite.

- As your own meteorologist, write the day's metaphorical forecast in your planning calendar. Be Proactive and purposeful about the weather you're choosing to carry throughout the day.

Day 1 Demonstrate Humility	**Day 2** Think Abundantly	**Day 3** Listen First	**Day 4** Declare Your Intent	**Day 5** Make and Keep Commitments
Day 6 Carry Your Own Weather	**Day 7** Inspire Trust	**Day 8** Model Work/Life Balance	**Day 9** Place the Right People in the Right Roles	**Day 10** Make Time for Relationships
Day 11 Check Your Paradigms	**Day 12** Lead Difficult Conversations	**Day 13** Talk Straight	**Day 14** Balance Courage and Consideration	**Day 15** Show Loyalty
Day 16 Make It Safe to Tell the Truth	**Day 17** Right Wrongs	**Day 18** Coach Continuously	**Day 19** Protect Your Team Against Urgencies	**Day 20** Hold Regular 1-on-1s
Day 21 Allow Others to Be Smart	**Day 22** Create Vision	**Day 23** Identify the Wildly Important Goals® (WIGs®)	**Day 24** Align Actions with the Wildly Important Goals	**Day 25** Ensure Your Systems Support Your Mission
Day 26 Deliver Results	**Day 27** Celebrate Wins	**Day 28** Make High-Value Decisions	**Day 29** Lead Through Change	**Day 30** Get Better

CHALLENGE 7

INSPIRE TRUST

Think of a person who had confidence in you and extended trust. Reflect on its ongoing impact. Will you have the same impact on your team members?

Trust is one of the most written-about and talked-about topics in the business world today. Ask yourself, *Am I more inclined to trust or distrust others?* Is your natural tendency to be suspicious of others, or are you able to extend trust even to those who have not yet fully "earned it"? As Abraham Lincoln famously said, "If you trust, you will be disappointed occasionally, but if you mistrust, you will be miserable all the time."

Any success I've achieved in life is the direct result of someone extending trust to me and in the process, allowing me to learn a critical leadership trait. A few immediately come to mind:

- Responsibility—Jane Begalla. Jane was my childhood neighbor who, when leaving for college, trusted me enough to hand over her treasured bakery stand at the local farmer's market. I ran it for several years, earning a nice income through high school.

- The desire to lead—Sam Romeo. Sam was my twelfth-grade teacher and the sponsor of the student government association. He believed in me, championed me, and inspired me to run in (and win) the election for student body president. (My theme was "It's Miller Time," clearly lifted without permission from the Miller Brewing Company).

- Hard work—Patrice Hobby and her then-husband Bill Hobby. Together they helped me become the youngest licensed realtor in my county and pushed me to sell my first property at the age of twenty. They also trusted me implicitly with their businesses, homes, cars… literally everything. Frankly, I sometimes abused it (let's just say a college-age party may or may not have occurred on the premises—and by "premises," I mean their expensive townhome). They continued to believe in me, even when I didn't deserve it.

- Vision—Frank Stansberry. Frank was my college public relations professor and my raving fan, and encouraged me to land an early internship at Disney, which in turn led to my first full-time career.

- Mentorship—Deborah Claesgens. Deborah was my first leader at the Disney Development Company. She was very tough on me, but I think she liked me more for who I could become and less for who I was: She placed enormous trust in me (sometimes blindly, I fear), and I owe my entire career to her.

- Showing courage—Bill Bennett. Bill was the leader who believed in me more than I ever believed in myself. You'll see Bill make an appearance in Challenge 15: Show Loyalty.

I could easily list dozens of people who extended significant trust to me throughout my life. I think I never fully appreciated all of them until I started writing this chapter.

There is one person in particular I want to highlight: Bob Guindon. He served as the leader of our international operations and transitioned FranklinCovey's U.K. office from licensee status to being company-owned. During this move, we faced rebuilding two decades' worth of processes, caring for dozens of clients, hiring salespeople, maintaining and growing revenue, and rebuilding systems.

Bob had apparently watched my performance in the Education Division and offered me the opportunity to move from Utah to the U.K. to help turn the office around. I can't describe my excitement. It was the type of thing you read about in someone else's book, not mine. I felt honored, important, humbled, and ecstatic.

I spent about nine months living in the U.K. and created such a management mess, I shudder to think about it. I suspect it was like a twenty-year-old Tony Robbins landing in a rural English town, entering an office of thirty prim and proper, set-in-their-ways professionals, all wondering what in the hell was happening. A tornado named Scott with a fatiguing "I can do anything and so can you!" American personality had just landed and couldn't seem to be contained.

I committed to multiple client meetings every day, when in fact I was late to or even missed many of them altogether, just trying to navigate roundabouts and dual carriageways (a fancy name for a highway), combined with driving a manual car, steering wheel on the left, all while traveling on the "opposite" side of the road.

> ANY SUCCESS I'VE ACHIEVED IN LIFE IS THE DIRECT RESULT OF SOMEONE EXTENDING TRUST AND ALLOWING ME TO LEARN A CRITICAL LEADERSHIP TRAIT.

When I wasn't causing havoc on the roads, I was disrupting every process inside the office. Creating direct-mail campaigns, organizing large client-engagement events, generally challenging every aspect of the status quo. In hindsight, my whirlwind no doubt created some momentum, but to what end, I'm not entirely certain.

The growth from my time in the U.K. was incalculable, even though I was considerably in over my head most of the time. That didn't appear to matter to Bob. I didn't know at the time that he was actually investing in me—not just for the U.K. transition, but for the future of the company. And for my own future as well, because great leaders do that. He extended trust beyond what I deserved, and the lasting impact has been instructive in my own leadership legacy. I attempt, at every opportunity, to extend trust to team members as it's been extended to me throughout my life.

FROM MESS TO SUCCESS:
INSPIRE TRUST

- I have a task for you—valuable enough that I've dedicated the following two pages to it. Many authors might suggest you take some time to do the following exercise outside of reading their book, but I want to implore you to do it right here, right now. Pay no mind to what you've been taught your entire life about writing in books and defacing property. This is *our* book, it's allowed to be a little messy—after all, that's my specialty.

- You'll notice the two pages after this are blank, save for some bullets. On the first page, I would like you to list all the people in your life who extended trust to you (write their names out as I did on page 58). To the side of their name, jot down a note that reminds you what their trust meant to you, maybe more now than it did then.

- When you have completed that list (it should be long if you're invested in it), complete the facing page to the right. Here, I'd encourage you to list the names of people on your team, in your division, organization, family, community, etc. Beside their name, write out what extending trust to them might look like— something you've not yet done. Jot down some actions, ideas, or projects that, with trust from you, they could potentially excel at. Be specific.

- Now, extend trust to them. The downside can't possibly be worse than the decision to send me to our U.K. office in transition.

THOSE WHO EXTENDED TRUST TO ME

-
-
-
-
-
-
-
-
-
-

THOSE TO WHOM I INTEND TO EXTEND TRUST

_____

-
-
-
-
-
-
-
-
-
-

Day 1 Demonstrate Humility	**Day 2** Think Abundantly	**Day 3** Listen First	**Day 4** Declare Your Intent	**Day 5** Make and Keep Commitments
Day 6 Carry Your Own Weather	**Day 7** Inspire Trust	**Day 8** Model Work/Life Balance	**Day 9** Place the Right People in the Right Roles	**Day 10** Make Time for Relationships
Day 11 Check Your Paradigms	**Day 12** Lead Difficult Conversations	**Day 13** Talk Straight	**Day 14** Balance Courage and Consideration	**Day 15** Show Loyalty
Day 16 Make It Safe to Tell the Truth	**Day 17** Right Wrongs	**Day 18** Coach Continuously	**Day 19** Protect Your Team Against Urgencies	**Day 20** Hold Regular 1-on-1s
Day 21 Allow Others to Be Smart	**Day 22** Create Vision	**Day 23** Identify the Wildly Important Goals® (WIGs®)	**Day 24** Align Actions with the Wildly Important Goals	**Day 25** Ensure Your Systems Support Your Mission
Day 26 Deliver Results	**Day 27** Celebrate Wins	**Day 28** Make High-Value Decisions	**Day 29** Lead Through Change	**Day 30** Get Better

CHALLENGE 8

MODEL WORK/LIFE BALANCE

If paparazzi had followed you last week, would they have seen a balance of activities at work and outside of work? What's the impact?

A secret is floating around the corporate world called "work/ life balance." It's a turn of phrase you're *supposed* to talk about as a vital company value. But the secret is that we don't mean it. Not really. It's well understood that, while we openly talk about structuring one's time and attention to effectively balance work and private life (wink, wink; nudge, nudge), if you *really* want to succeed as a leader, you clock as many hours as you can—be the first to arrive at the office and the last to leave, life balance be damned. For those of you who think the tide has turned, according to research published in 2018, *The Project: Time Off* survey, 24 percent of Americans reported they hadn't taken a vacation in more than a year, and 52 percent reported having unused vacation days at the end of 2017.

It wasn't always this way. Thirty years ago, my father was a mid-level leader at a Fortune 500 company. I only remember his office calling him at home once or twice during the evening—over the course of three decades. His boss never called him at home. Until the early '90s, no matter your level, work was finished when you left the office. Sure, you thought about it, but you weren't expected to engage until the next workday (and you certainly weren't focused on it over the weekend).

We seem to have lost that old-school wisdom over the years. To my mind, without the energizing and renewing activities that take place outside the office, you can't be "whole" or fulfilled. And if you're not fulfilled in multiple areas of your life, you likely won't be as productive at work. Studies even link an active sex life to improved job satisfaction and engagement at work (to clarify, not an active sex life *at* work). The point is, the more fulfilled you are, the more productive you'll be. And the more productive you are, the fewer hours you'll have to clock at work. Conversely, the more miserable you are, the less productive you'll be, thus requiring more hours at the office to get things done. It's a vicious or virtuous cycle, depending on where you jump on.

It took me a while to figure this out. Have I mastered it? Not even close. I've got a good deal of muscle memory around saying yes, taking on the big lifts, accepting the keynote on the other side of the world, etc. And let's be honest, thanks to technology, it's never been more difficult to find work/life balance—and it will only get worse. The line between work and life is mostly blurred beyond distinction. Sure, I know people who proudly announce their militant adherence to strict work/life boundaries. They're the same ones who, after a dinner out, itemize the check and pay their 41 percent because you had two glasses of wine and they had one. I wish them well in their commitment to hardcore balance. *Separate checks, please… separate tables also.*

As nearly every private enterprise needs a global presence to compete, the expectation is only increasing that we use our technology to stay connected and engaged. Often in exchange for being constantly available, many of us are afforded more flexible work environments. In fact, many companies have adopted a flexible vacation policy for salaried associates: "Take what you need, but deliver your results."

DON'T FORGET, IT'S YOUR LIFE, SO DON'T SPEND IT ALL AT WORK.

Sounds like a reasonable tit for tat. But pardon the phrase, I'd bet there's more tat ("but deliver your results") than tit ("take what you need in vacation"). How many of you took more than ten vacation days in the past calendar year (and don't count government holidays)? I can tell you I didn't, and it isn't because I couldn't think of anywhere to go or anything to do. I was either acting out of my habit of saying yes, or continuing to labor under the delusion that taking time off would make me less productive, not more. Welcome to my management mess. I realize this paradigm may be more American-centric, but the world isn't becoming less competitive, so govern your careers accordingly.

There's a reason we call this challenge "Model" Work/Life Balance, not just "be an advocate for" it. When leaders themselves don't have a life, they not only look pitiful in the eyes of their teams, they also set a very low standard for how others behave, consciously or unconsciously.

Don't forget, it's *your* life, so don't spend it all at work. To quote countless people, nobody on their deathbed ever wished they'd spent more time at the office. No one can dictate the right balance—you decide. We all have different values (personal and professional), different seasons in our careers, financial demands, skills, fears, etc. Let no one else decide what you value. I don't feel the need to take your time and further advocate *why* you should be balanced and take time in your life. That's readily apparent to all of us, based on all the literature advocating it. What I want to spend the time on now is, as a leader, why it's important for you to model it for others.

Beyond investing in yourself, what you model is likely what you will see come to life in your colleagues. Your people need to know that it's safe for them to take time off. Whether or not you think your own behavior translates to theirs, trust me, it does. Your team members will draw conclusions about what is acceptable and what is not, based both on what you say and what you do. If you truly want your people to live balanced lives that allow them a sense of renewal, purpose, and increased productivity in the workplace, you have to model it yourself.

LIFE BALANCE DOESN'T NECESSARILY MEAN TAKING A VACATION. LEADERS NEED TO TAKE TIME OFF TO INVEST IN THEMSELVES, DEVELOP HOBBIES, AND WORK ON THEIR HEALTH AND RELATIONSHIPS. WE ALSO NEED TO BECOME MORE MULTIDIMENSIONAL BY NOT LETTING OUR JOBS DEFINE US. WE'VE ALL EXPERIENCED SEASONS IN OUR LIVES THAT LEAN MORE TOWARD OUR CAREERS AND THAT'S OKAY, AS LONG AS IT'S LIMITED TO A SEASON. REMEMBER, SEASONS PASS, OR AT LEAST THEY SHOULD.

Life balance doesn't necessarily mean taking a vacation. Leaders need to take time off to invest in themselves, develop hobbies, and work on their health and relationships. We also need to become more multidimensional by not letting our jobs define us. We've all experienced seasons in our lives that lean more toward our careers—and that's okay, as long as it's limited to a season. Remember, seasons pass, or at least they should.

Never use the excuse that if you take time off, you'll just face an increasingly daunting workload when you return. That is likely true for all of us. But that lame logic could also be applied to showering—never take one, because you're just going to get dirty again.

If you really don't want a vacation, or truly can't afford one, there's no shame in that. Some who are single or have limited social groups may not want to travel alone. Others with large financial pressures frankly don't want to increase that stress by trying to force a vacation into the budget. It's your business, but don't let these become excuses for staying yoked to your job. Announce you're taking a week off and simply leave. It may in fact be a "staycation," and that's fine. Sit at home, draw the shades, and start crocheting. Do not call, text, or email any associates. Remember, your team members also benefit from a "boss break."

If nothing else, not taking vacations makes you look pitiful. People will talk about it. That's horrible for your brand. Worse yet, your team won't aspire to your job. (Who wants to follow your example?) Better to disappear for a week and make something up about visiting Rome. Here come the emails about me encouraging you to lie, but if it gets you out of the office, then it's worth the inbox barrage.

FROM MESS TO SUCCESS:
MODEL WORK/LIFE BALANCE

- Recognize that the most influential people live balanced lives.

- Make a list of easy-to-implement things you could do to bring better balance.

- Discuss openly with your team the real pressures everyone faces to grow their careers and enjoy their lives. Make it safe for everyone to take the time they need to do both.

- Be vulnerable about the fact that work/life balance is also a challenge for you. Everyone desires authenticity and relatability in their leader.

  1. Brainstorm with your team the observable behaviors that would indicate the proper work/life balance has been reached. Implement and champion them.
  2. Invite colleagues to be open and honest if they feel that things have moved too far to either extreme.

- Take time off to renew, and encourage team members to do the same.

- Welcome them back by showing genuine interest in what they did, learned, or enjoyed.

PART 2

LEAD OTHERS

Day 1 Demonstrate Humility	**Day 2** Think Abundantly	**Day 3** Listen First	**Day 4** Declare Your Intent	**Day 5** Make and Keep Commitments
Day 6 Carry Your Own Weather	**Day 7** Inspire Trust	**Day 8** Model Work/Life Balance	**Day 9** Place the Right People in the Right Roles	**Day 10** Make Time for Relationships
Day 11 Check Your Paradigms	**Day 12** Lead Difficult Conversations	**Day 13** Talk Straight	**Day 14** Balance Courage and Consideration	**Day 15** Show Loyalty
Day 16 Make It Safe to Tell the Truth	**Day 17** Right Wrongs	**Day 18** Coach Continuously	**Day 19** Protect Your Team Against Urgencies	**Day 20** Hold Regular 1-on-1s
Day 21 Allow Others to Be Smart	**Day 22** Create Vision	**Day 23** Identify the Wildly Important Goals® (WIGs®)	**Day 24** Align Actions with the Wildly Important Goals	**Day 25** Ensure Your Systems Support Your Mission
Day 26 Deliver Results	**Day 27** Celebrate Wins	**Day 28** Make High-Value Decisions	**Day 29** Lead Through Change	**Day 30** Get Better

CHALLENGE 9

PLACE THE RIGHT PEOPLE IN THE RIGHT ROLES

How many people on your team are in the right role? Do you need to make adjustments?

Putting the right people in the right roles is often more complex than it seems. Managing talent can be like a game of chess—strategies are implemented, reality takes a turn, and your best-laid plans can fall apart with one wrong move. How you approach placing people in their roles is often the most complicated aspect of your job: who to hire and who to pass on, who to promote and where to place them, when to move them again and when not to, and whether you need to encourage them (or directly tell them it's time) to leave.

BUILDING A WINNING TEAM CAN BE ONE OF YOUR GREATEST LEGACIES AS A LEADER, BUT IT'S RARELY RECOGNIZED OR REWARDED IN REAL TIME. IN FACT, YOU'LL LIKELY ONLY GET CREDIT FOR IT AFTER THE TEAM DISBANDS OR YOU'VE MOVED ON.

Chances are you've seen what happens when someone with the talents of a chess queen gets stuck playing as a rook (or worse yet, a pawn!). I know a person who, in my estimation, is as close to a genius as I'll ever meet. I'm not referring to having a brain for quantum physics, but having an unbounded level of creativity and idea generation. This very seasoned and exceedingly charismatic colleague ("Brandon") had at least four separate roles leading four separate teams in the same organization. Graciously put, he also had a legacy of consistently falling short of success. And this is despite him being well-intended, possessing enthusiasm beyond measure, having a clear vision, and demonstrating a work ethic that inspired even me. (And I'm known as the Energizer Bunny—even *after* 5:00 p.m.!) Brandon was never in the right role.

You likely know someone in the same position—misaligned, or not reporting to a leader who could marshal their energies toward the highest-leveraged projects. When a person is consistently in the wrong role, they tend to bounce around a lot (and not because they accomplished the mission). I can recall many examples from my experience—some successes, other failures, but all well-intended hires and promotions:

- The twenty-year associate who performed well, but mostly flew under the radar. That is, until a leader moved them into a vital company initiative that leveraged their deep expertise and knowledge. Their high performance is now generating an unprecedented level of positive career exposure.

- The highly competent individual contributor who launched many successful initiatives. Now, moved to a broad leadership role, they're struggling to gain influence with their direct reports.

- The newly promoted individual contributor, now leading their former peers and implementing significant improvements companywide.

- The long-term associate performing well in one division, then hired by a different type of leader for a similar role. As this new leader provides more exciting challenges and direction, the associate's influence and confidence suddenly grows at an exponential rate.

- A highly credentialed technical expert in their field who never fully assimilates into the company culture or understands the business model. Their time in their role is short, and they point a finger at others as the reason for their departure, when they could have had significant impact with better collaboration and coaching from their leader.

Business author and leadership expert Jim Collins famously wrote in *Good to Great*, "Get the right people on the bus, the wrong people off the bus, and the right people in the right seats." Building a winning team can be one of your greatest legacies as a leader, but it's rarely recognized or rewarded in real time. In fact, you'll likely only get credit for it after the team disbands or you've moved on.

The challenge for leaders is that there's no shortcut (that I know of) to guarantee you've got the right people in the right roles. I think of it as a "years in the saddle" thing, meaning it takes a good deal of mistakes and even falling off. You have to pick yourself up and take the reins again. This isn't a skill you're born with—there's no workshop or list of absolute best practices to follow. It's an art, not a science—you earn it by learning and living it. I know a person in our company who has been with us for fifteen years and is in their seventh role. And everyone agrees, the seventh role is the right one. Thank goodness we (and she) took the time to figure it out and get it right. It doesn't mean this person was wrong in her previous roles, but rather that she's fully found her voice, she's the right person in the right seat, and the organization is reaping extraordinary rewards. She also seems more fulfilled, more valued, and happier than I've seen her before.

To accelerate the process of getting the right person into the right role, carefully consider these questions:

- What skills and passions does this person have, and what type of team can make the most of them?

- What kind of leader will help this person flourish and tap into their strengths?

- What types of personalities will this person struggle to work with, and can you address it early, make it safe to talk about, and help ensure success?

- What systems and processes will help this person thrive in their new role? Are they used to bootstrapping and fixing things themselves, or used to large infrastructures and deep resources to call upon?

- What culture will this person experience in their new role? Are they nimble enough to assimilate into a strong culture, or are they influential enough to lead and breed a new and better culture?

- Is this person moving from an individual contributor to a leadership role? Are they able to identify, and perhaps let go of, some of the traits that made them successful and learn new skills to inspire and lead others? Are you in a position to help coach this person and help them be successful?

- What are the seemingly small, self-defeating traits you've noticed in this individual? Can considerate and courageous coaching minimize them or even turn them into assets?

- Which changes could you make in your own style to better ensure their success and impact in their new role?

Successful leaders often discover they're much like the eHarmony of business—they embrace the art of matchmaking and introducing the right people to the right roles. This is a hard-earned competence of mine that truly didn't come until a decade into my formal leadership experience. Many leaders will have to fail their way to eventual success at this; the key is how fast can you get there with as few divorces as possible.

While we're on the topic, ask yourself: "Am *I* in the right role? How do I know? Is there another division, team, or leader that could better develop my skills and broaden my own influence?" Don't be reluctant to ask these questions of yourself and, maybe even more important, of your own leader.

FROM MESS TO SUCCESS:

PLACE THE RIGHT PEOPLE IN THE RIGHT ROLES

- Identify someone's true passions and strengths so you can align those to your business needs.

- Use the list of questions in this challenge to assess whether someone could play a different role.

- Seek others' ideas about your observations and opinions.

- Have courageous conversations to address situations around personality, emotional maturity, self-awareness, etc. (By the way, too many leaders skip this bullet and move on to the next.)

- Exercise the courage to remedy any misalignments.

Day 1 Demonstrate Humility	**Day 2** Think Abundantly	**Day 3** Listen First	**Day 4** Declare Your Intent	**Day 5** Make and Keep Commitments
Day 6 Carry Your Own Weather	**Day 7** Inspire Trust	**Day 8** Model Work/Life Balance	**Day 9** Place the Right People in the Right Roles	**Day 10** Make Time for Relationships
Day 11 Check Your Paradigms	**Day 12** Lead Difficult Conversations	**Day 13** Talk Straight	**Day 14** Balance Courage and Consideration	**Day 15** Show Loyalty
Day 16 Make It Safe to Tell the Truth	**Day 17** Right Wrongs	**Day 18** Coach Continuously	**Day 19** Protect Your Team Against Urgencies	**Day 20** Hold Regular 1-on-1s
Day 21 Allow Others to Be Smart	**Day 22** Create Vision	**Day 23** Identify the Wildly Important Goals® (WIGs®)	**Day 24** Align Actions with the Wildly Important Goals	**Day 25** Ensure Your Systems Support Your Mission
Day 26 Deliver Results	**Day 27** Celebrate Wins	**Day 28** Make High-Value Decisions	**Day 29** Lead Through Change	**Day 30** Get Better

CHALLENGE 10

MAKE TIME FOR RELATIONSHIPS

Do you practice the principle that, with
people, slow is fast and fast is slow?

Envision the breakfast buffet at your favorite hotel. A loaf of uninspiring sliced bread often sits next to the semi-warm Danish, waiting to be toasted. For the larger hotels, a mere toaster won't suffice—they need one of those toaster conveyors. You lay your bread on the metal wire and, in about forty-five seconds, it spits the bread onto the bottom tray, perfectly toasted.

> I PUT MOST OF MY ENCOUNTERS INTO A METAPHORICAL TOASTER AND DIAL IT TO "FAST." IT'S BEEN MY IMPULSIVE, IMPETUOUS, EFFICIENT PERSONALITY TO TREAT PEOPLE LIKE TOAST. GUESS HOW IT'S WORKED OUT? CRUMBY. (PUN INTENDED).

This process has never worked for me—not once.

Why? When it's my turn to send my bread through, I instinctively spin the dial to the fastest setting. It's not that I want light toast; it's just that I can't chemically, biologically, or physically stand in front of the painfully slow machine while it chugs along at a mind-numbing pace. I turn it to the maximum, try to rush it, and end up with (surprise!) slightly warm bread.

Welcome to my relationships with people. I put most of my encounters into a metaphorical toaster and dial it to *"fast."* It's been my impulsive, impetuous, efficient personality to treat people like toast. Guess how it's worked out? Crumby (pun intended).

Thankfully, I received an important lesson in making time for people from Chuck Farnsworth, one of my first corporate leaders and mentors. It happened early in my professional career while I was working as a frontline salesperson for our Education Division. I sold leadership-development solutions to colleges and universities, and Chuck was our founding vice president. We had a big dinner with the vice president of administration at Ohio State University and her team. This VP was at the top of her game: she'd come from a Fortune 50 company to run the physical plants, ground crews, and innumerable other functions at one of the largest universities in the United States.

My plan was simple: crank the toast machine to "fast" and push the huge sell through. And when I say huge, I mean HUGE—this was a big deal for our Education Division and to me personally. Luckily, I was a twenty-something salesman with plenty of charisma and the braggadocio to get it done. As soon as we were seated at the table, I ordered appetizers for the group. No sense wasting time finding out what dishes people wanted (or might be allergic to). I had it all under control. I was a guided missile set to "sell." In retrospect, I have to wonder what those seasoned team members must have thought of me.

I launched into my business conversation right away, hoping to push our pending sale to a verbal commitment. Then, early into my highly polished routine, I vividly remember Chuck placing his hand on my knee under the table, tightening his grip in a wholly appropriate attempt to save me from myself. I hit the brakes, not knowing what Chuck wanted, but sensing I was off track. He then effortlessly redirected the conversation to mutual interests, our families, and any areas where we could sincerely connect with our client—areas that had nothing to do with the prospective sale. I'll let you guess whether we ended up signing the deal.

Chuck is a master at making time for relationships; not because he's slick, sly, or practiced, but because he genuinely cares about people—their successes and their challenges. His sales philosophy is simple: In the process of learning more about others and their needs, if he can help them by selling them one of our solutions, then great! Let's do business. If not, let's part ways and maybe I could recommend another solution provider that would be a better fit. He's hands-down the most effective person I've ever known when it comes to working with people—a skill required of every leader.

To be clear, my struggle with this challenge doesn't mean I inherently undervalue relationships. I just like to speed them along at a brisk pace! I also make no apologies for my productivity in life. Plainly said, I like to accomplish things. I enjoy working hard and pushing others to great accomplishments. I love deadlines, and I'm known for getting things done with annoying urgency. I will probably never be asked to deliver a eulogy or a Thanksgiving prayer, but I'd be the first asked to help evacuate a burning building. You might need therapy afterward, but I promise to get you out alive!

I'm still learning to slow down—way down—when it comes to others. As Dr. Covey liked to say, "With people, slow is fast and fast is slow."

Here's an illustration of this principle that's had a profound impact on me. Each morning I buy several newspapers from a hotel gift shop near my home. The lady who worked the counter for some years was what I'd call equal parts seasoned and salty. Well up in years, with a hard-to-place accent, it seemed like she should have retired long before. Our habit was to exchange brief pleasantries as she scanned my papers, ran my card, and commented on how expensive it all was. I would offer a quick smile and hurry out.

On numerous occasions, I watched as this woman struggled with the credit-card machine, was short with customers, or got flustered if someone wanted to return something. It happened so often, in fact, that I became increasingly annoyed by what I viewed as a lack of competence and poor attitude on her part. I even considered suggesting to a manager that perhaps it was time for her to "move on."

Then one morning, while going through our usual routine, this woman announced that the next day would be her last: she was finally retiring and moving back to France to live with her daughter. I was a bit surprised at that (I didn't think her accent was French), but my "fast" setting pushed me to get back into my morning routine. I quickly muttered some kind of congratulations and left.

I thought about our brief conversation a few more times that day, unsure why the interaction kept returning to me even well into the evening. With people, slow is fast and fast is slow. I had been nothing but fast with this woman over a countless number of encounters. I wondered what the cost was.

The next morning, with my empathy and focus on "high," my eight-year-old son and I grabbed a bouquet from a grocery-store cooler and drove to the hotel gift shop. The moment we walked in, my son handed her the arrangement. She was visibly stunned. Then I really listened to her for the first time. In that small moment of making time for the relationship, I learned more in five minutes than I had in the previous year. She uncharacteristically disclosed she was turning eighty that month, had worked at the hotel for thirteen years, and had lived in the U.S. since she was fifty. She was born in Rhodesia (now Zimbabwe) and grew up a white girl in a black-majority culture. She shared how her parents had instilled in her an unflinching work ethic (which is why she was still working, even though she could have stopped long ago) and how she had bought her first bicycle at age ten with her own money. She was excited to spend time with her daughter in France, but as she continued (tears streaming down her face), she confessed how scared she was about the future.

REAL RELATIONSHIPS REQUIRE US TO SLOW DOWN, EVEN WHEN EVERYTHING AROUND US IS DEMANDING WE GO FASTER. BUT LIKE MY TOAST (OR LACK THEREOF), OUR EFFECTIVENESS AS LEADERS (AND PARENTS) REQUIRES US TO TAKE THE TIME TO GET IT RIGHT.

Her story (which I can't do justice to here) amounted to an amazing woman with a remarkable life. Because I had never even thought to slow down and take time for her, I had missed out on a much more meaningful relationship, if only for a few minutes each morning. But at the very least, we didn't part company that way.

Each morning, as I buy my papers from the gift shop, I find myself hoping she is doing well.

Twenty years ago, my perpetual "fast" selling would have stayed in place. But today I'm working at it (and trying to share that lesson with my three sons).

Real relationships require us to slow down, even when everything around us is demanding we go faster. But like my toast (or lack thereof), our effectiveness as leaders (and parents) requires us to take the time to get it right.

FROM MESS TO SUCCESS:
MAKE TIME FOR RELATIONSHIPS

- Ask yourself: Is your default setting "fast"? If yes, is that shortchanging you and others? Is your efficiency mindset undercutting a more beneficial effectiveness mindset?

- Understand that there's no such thing as developing a relationship "efficiently." Trust, respect, and rapport take time and investment.

- Intentionally slow down and connect with others in ways they prefer.

- Commit to ask a team member or colleague how he or she is doing and really listen to their response. When appropriate, sincerely explore their answer.

- Recognize your judgments regarding time:

  1. Do you give time to people or situations you can't equate with productivity or value?
  2. Are your exchanges focused on gathering information or on strengthening relationships? Commit to make them both.

Day 1	Day 2	Day 3	Day 4	Day 5
Demonstrate Humility	Think Abundantly	Listen First	Declare Your Intent	Make and Keep Commitments
Day 6	Day 7	Day 8	Day 9	Day 10
Carry Your Own Weather	Inspire Trust	Model Work/Life Balance	Place the Right People in the Right Roles	Make Time for Relationships
Day 11	Day 12	Day 13	Day 14	Day 15
Check Your Paradigms	Lead Difficult Conversations	Talk Straight	Balance Courage and Consideration	Show Loyalty
Day 16	Day 17	Day 18	Day 19	Day 20
Make It Safe to Tell the Truth	Right Wrongs	Coach Continuously	Protect Your Team Against Urgencies	Hold Regular 1-on-1s
Day 21	Day 22	Day 23	Day 24	Day 25
Allow Others to Be Smart	Create Vision	Identify the Wildly Important Goals® (WIGs®)	Align Actions with the Wildly Important Goals	Ensure Your Systems Support Your Mission
Day 26	Day 27	Day 28	Day 29	Day 30
Deliver Results	Celebrate Wins	Make High-Value Decisions	Lead Through Change	Get Better

CHALLENGE 11

CHECK YOUR PARADIGMS

Are you seeing people and situations accurately?

You've been lied to your entire life. Some lies are small, told to you as you watch a television drama or a film at the movie theater. We're okay with being lied to in that way—so much so, that there's even a term for it: suspension of disbelief. We come to a kind of agreement with the director: If you promise to entertain me, I'll promise to stop *disbelieving* in aliens and a hero who can single-handedly save the universe. We accept these little lies as harmless entertainment. Other lies are bigger, frequently told by us about others and their intentions. There's a term for that kind of lie too: fundamental attribution error. One of the reasons we allow these bigger lies into our lives is that we don't stop and check our paradigms.

Dr. Covey popularized the term "paradigm," which comes from the Greek root *paradigma,* meaning a pattern, model, or representation of something. Our paradigms are the perceptions, frames of reference, worldviews, value systems, or lenses through which we see everyone and everything, including ourselves. They add meaning, true or false, to the world around us, and affect the way we interpret what we see and experience, and how we interact and relate with others.

OUR PARADIGMS ARE PERHAPS THE MOST POWERFUL TOOLS WE HAVE IN HOW WE INTERACT WITH OTHERS. IT'S WORTH SERIOUS INTROSPECTION TO CHECK WHY WE VIEW OTHERS THE WAY WE DO AND CORRECT ANY MISPERCEPTIONS OR OUTDATED BELIEFS.

I once had a fairly successful friend in the movie industry who had lots of credits to her name, working mostly on the production side of both movies and television. This friend once said something in passing that I'm sure she would never remember (and while she likely didn't offer it with the same gravitas I received it, I've pondered her words for three decades now). When referring to an up-and-coming actor, she remarked, "I knew them when they were nothing." It was a phrase I'd hear her repeat about other actors as well.

Now, it wasn't the fact that her words were particularly unkind or mean-spirited that stuck with me, but that they exposed one of her paradigms. Over her career, this former friend had worked with numerous famous individuals. Many had started out as proverbial starving artists, performing in community theaters and living hand-to-mouth before working their way up to fame and wealth (unlike you and me, who were catapulted into the C-suite without hard work or experience; I highly recommend this second strategy—please email me at scott.miller@franklincovey.com and tell me how it worked for you). Her operating paradigm seemed to be that nobody really earned their success.

They were forever tethered to how they started, which is absurd because we all started from somewhere—except for royalty, and my sense is that many of them want out. The power of that paradigm shaped her thoughts, actions, and beliefs regarding many people she knew. She had a fixed paradigm about who people were when they "started" instead of who they eventually became. My personal management mess appeared when I fell into the same limiting trap.

I'd worked with "Andy" for over a decade, and we had formed a friendship outside of our professional lives. We attended family birthday parties, traded career challenges over the backyard BBQ, and I genuinely thought of him as someone I both respected and trusted. But despite our friendship and our long working history, we had a rather public falling-out (one of less than a handful in my entire life, but painful nonetheless).

When I first met Andy, he was a junior entry-level associate—young, competent, fun, and hardworking. Because I was both older and more senior to him in the company, I based part of my paradigm on the organizational pecking order: *My rung on the career ladder is higher than yours*. And let's face it: a good portion of my self-esteem was tied to my place on the ladder, so having a few rungs between us felt safe, at least to me.

The problem with this paradigm was that Andy was getting promoted through his hard work, successfully delivered projects, and refined professional skills. All the while, I never checked my paradigm or became introspective about why hierarchy mattered so much to me. Our falling-out had to do with the inevitable collision between my outdated paradigm and a new reality.

How arrogant of me.

It came to a head when Andy, now working directly on a project for the CEO, asked for "in-progress" work samples from my team. I'm the first to admit Andy was simply doing his job and executing on what the CEO had asked him to do. This was all well and good, but I had a long-standing policy of NEVER showing "in-progress" work because it rarely, if ever, produced a good outcome with the CEO. The nature of my team's projects benefited from stakeholders seeing a finished or near-finished product, rather than having to try to visualize and understand how the "work in progress" would ultimately come together. Where my paradigm got me into a mess wasn't the nature of the request (generally reasonable), but the fact that I viewed Andy as my "junior." So instead of explaining my point of view and offering to go to the CEO to better understand the nature of the request, I took it as a subordinate disrespecting my process. I reacted harshly, shutting him down publicly in front of my team and sending him on his way empty-handed.

For whatever reason, my paradigm about Andy and his role had remained rigidly locked into place. That's no excuse for how I behaved, but it does help me understand *why* I behaved the way I did and the need for me to change.

Later that day, and over the course of the next few days, I tried to apologize, but our relationship had fractured beyond repair. With the benefit of hindsight, it became glaringly obvious that paradigms may start out true, but can often lose their veracity over time. You don't have to have a negative view to end up with an inaccurate paradigm. A paradigm can be a snapshot in time. Go too long without checking it, and you may fail to recognize how people (and even the world) have changed around you. That was a hard lesson to learn, sadly, for us both.

Fortunately for Andy, he didn't need me to succeed and has gone on to be a high-contributing associate in the organization. And I've worked hard to be mindful of how I view others, situations, and the nature of the paradigms I hold. I can honestly report I'm better at this than I once was.

Our paradigms are perhaps the most powerful tools we have in how we interact with others. It's worth serious introspection to check why we view others the way we do and correct any misperceptions or outdated beliefs.

FROM MESS TO SUCCESS:
CHECK YOUR PARADIGMS

- Make a list of all the people who report to you. One by one, reflect on your current paradigm of them as a professional or their promotability. Are you willing to challenge its accuracy? Could it be incomplete?

- If you were to suspend your current paradigm of someone, could they earn their way to a different paradigm? If so, how? What would you need to "see"?

- Flip this challenge onto yourself. Seek out a trusted friend or colleague and ask them to share their paradigm about you—as a leader, friend, colleague, or any other role they may have context for. Can you summon the maturity and introspection to grow into the paradigm you'd like them to hold?

- Checking paradigms often requires a sustained, deep look into yourself to work. This is not a "quick fix." Ask yourself: *Am I willing to pay the price to change my mindset?*

Day 1 Demonstrate Humility	**Day 2** Think Abundantly	**Day 3** Listen First	**Day 4** Declare Your Intent	**Day 5** Make and Keep Commitments
Day 6 Carry Your Own Weather	**Day 7** Inspire Trust	**Day 8** Model Work/Life Balance	**Day 9** Place the Right People in the Right Roles	**Day 10** Make Time for Relationships
Day 11 Check Your Paradigms	**Day 12** Lead Difficult Conversations	**Day 13** Talk Straight	**Day 14** Balance Courage and Consideration	**Day 15** Show Loyalty
Day 16 Make It Safe to Tell the Truth	**Day 17** Right Wrongs	**Day 18** Coach Continuously	**Day 19** Protect Your Team Against Urgencies	**Day 20** Hold Regular 1-on-1s
Day 21 Allow Others to Be Smart	**Day 22** Create Vision	**Day 23** Identify the Wildly Important Goals® (WIGs®)	**Day 24** Align Actions with the Wildly Important Goals	**Day 25** Ensure Your Systems Support Your Mission
Day 26 Deliver Results	**Day 27** Celebrate Wins	**Day 28** Make High-Value Decisions	**Day 29** Lead Through Change	**Day 30** Get Better

CHALLENGE 12

LEAD DIFFICULT CONVERSATIONS

Have you avoided a difficult conversation and inadvertently caused the situation to worsen?

As a leader, you likely get to do some cool stuff. Depending on your organizational culture, span of control, budget, and responsibility, you can have a real impact and learn a lot along the way. You likely:

- Interview and hire new associates.

- Coach and see improvement in team members.

- Offer praise and feedback to high performers.

- Design strategy and break company—or even industry—norms.

- Recognize success and bestow awards and incentives.

- Order in lunch and celebrate team wins.

- Create the meeting agendas and lead the conversation.

- Assign projects as you choose.

> ...IF YOU DON'T LEAD DIFFICULT CONVERSATIONS, STEP DOWN. IMMEDIATELY. CALL YOUR LEADER AND TELL THEM YOU CAN'T CONTINUE IN THE ROLE ANY LONGER. LET SOMEONE ELSE TAKE OVER. (YOU CAN EVEN LEAVE YOUR WORD-OF-THE-DAY CALENDAR FOR YOUR REPLACEMENT.)

No doubt there's fun and enjoyment in your role. But—and you knew there was a "but" lingering out there—there's an area of leadership that's so daunting for so many that they avoid it; yet, if you don't add it to the above list, you frankly don't deserve your job. I'll even take it a step further: If you don't do it, step down. Immediately. Call your leader and tell them you can't continue in the role any longer. Let someone else take over. (You can even leave your word-of-the-day calendar for your replacement.)

The leadership challenge I'm referring to is your ability to lead difficult conversations.

Having to fire someone is a difficult conversation. Giving tough feedback is a difficult conversation. Finding a way to tell a colleague that their cologne is reminiscent of a wildebeest with questionable dietary habits is a difficult conversation. Regardless of the topic, difficult conversations share two traits: they're hard and they suck. Yet, if you *really* want to be a leader (and it's okay if you decide you don't), leading difficult conversations is not something you can neglect, even if you're convinced you can work around them or they're not that important, given your long to-do list.

People who have worked with me believe I'm comfortable with these conversations because I inherited some gene that allows me to easily and freely discuss common "undiscussables." I can't count the number of times associates, friends, and peers (and my wife) have said, "But it's so easy for *you* to tell someone that!"

Here's my response: Bullsh#t.

Contrary to popular belief, I didn't come out of the womb telling colleagues they weren't collaborative or needed to apologize to someone they wronged. I didn't just fall into the skill of closing the door and telling someone they were offensive in a meeting or that their overly long presentation featured the interjection "um" thirty-seven times. The skill of leading difficult conversations comes with practice. And lots of awkward attempts and outright failures. I could finish this chapter with story after story of failures so terrible and haunting you'd never even consider stepping up to the responsibility. That's not the point. The point is that any difficult leadership skill requires a gym and muscle-building analogy, so here I go: If you want biceps (and oh, I do), there's no shortcut—you've got to do the reps, baby. Now apply that to whatever sport you're into, forget that I called you "baby," and we can move on.

You have to practice, role-play, and rehearse these conversations repeatedly. You'll get better over time, and it won't be so awful. But here's the part you probably didn't expect: there's a strong possibility you'll provide someone the kind of insight nobody has ever offered them before. Think about that for a moment. You, as a leader, can break lifelong habits, shine a light on blind spots, and help someone change their brand for the better. Unlike the countless other leaders who are well-intentioned but never exercise the courage to be honest, you can change the entire trajectory of someone's life. Now that's leadership in action.

If you're willing to allow for such a possibility, I guarantee it will change the way you think about leading difficult conversations. There's an art to delivering feedback that unequivocally makes the necessary points and keeps a colleague's self-esteem and self-confidence intact. What's the secret? Let me suggest three things: good intent, practice, and learning from the experts. There's no easy answer to getting better at leading difficult conversations. First, check your intent and ensure you have their best interest at heart. No practiced technique matters if your intent is ill-founded. Second, find someone you trust, and practice without revealing names or other sensitive specifics. Role-play the difficult conversation, get feedback, and then role-play it again.

The third way to master the art of difficult conversations is to learn from the experts. There are good resources out there, and at FranklinCovey, we teach a series of "dos and don'ts" as well. These include:

- Don't get stuck in the preparation phase. Practice is vital, but don't use it as an excuse not to hold the real conversation.

- Don't use comparative language: "You should write your reports the way Emily does."

- Don't assume you have all the facts. It's possible there's a story behind the story, and while it may not change the feedback you offer, the additional context may change how you deliver it.

- Do Think Win-Win. Make sure your motives are genuine.

- Do describe your concerns. Use terms like "I was surprised to hear…" or "I'm concerned about…"

- Do give specific examples. Focus on facts versus your opinions.

- Do listen. Concentrate and reflect on the way the other person feels.

- Do ask open-ended questions: "People are perceiving you this way—can you tell me why you think that's happening?"

- Do be as specific as possible without violating the person's privacy. It's a delicate balance that requires sophistication and genuine care.

Successful leaders can learn to lead difficult conversations from colleagues who are senior, peers, other team members, and specialists. Sit down and share the situation with someone at the right organizational level; ask how they'd handle the conversation. And when it comes to the tenor of the dialogue, I like to think about how, where, and when *I'd* like the news delivered to me.

Give yourself permission to make mistakes and learn this skill. You'll screw up a few difficult conversations, guaranteed. That means you must apologize for the wrong word choice or tone or speed. You might even open the conversation with the sincere statement, *"I'm sure I will say this wrong, so please forgive me in advance if I stumble, but there's a sensitive topic we need to talk about…"*

You can also get advice from Human Resources. I've chosen to outsource a few high-stakes conversations to HR completely, given the topic or other sensitive issue, but this is a rarity. In my experience, you need to own 95 percent of the conversations yourself. As I look back at my personal leadership highlights thus far, many of them begin with someone saying to me (long after the intervention), "Scott, you were the only person in my career who had the courage to tell me..."

At the beginning of this section, I wrote that leading difficult conversations is so important that, if you aren't willing to do it, you should step down from your leadership role. Hopefully, now you know *why*: it's the one conversation with the potential and power to completely change someone's life for the better—or the worse, if not done right or avoided altogether.

One final thought. Any "gutless wonder" can deliver harsh news or feedback. It takes diplomacy, empathy, and thoughtfulness to ensure that the difficult conversation keeps the receiver's self-esteem strongly intact, while giving them hope and a path forward on how to improve.

FROM MESS TO SUCCESS:
LEAD DIFFICULT CONVERSATIONS

- Identify a difficult conversation you need to hold.

- If you've been delaying it, have an honest conversation with yourself about why. Is it the nature of your relationship with the other person? your discomfort with the topic? your skill and confidence in communicating it appropriately? Pinpoint the root cause and address that first.

- Identify a more seasoned leader with whom you can role-play the conversation. Be aware of sensitive information and confidentiality.

- Take a moment and challenge your paradigm—are you viewing the issue holistically? Have you gathered all the relevant facts? Have you considered the other person's point of view, and are you open-minded about the path forward?

Day 1	Day 2	Day 3	Day 4	Day 5
Demonstrate Humility	Think Abundantly	Listen First	Declare Your Intent	Make and Keep Commitments
Day 6	**Day 7**	**Day 8**	**Day 9**	**Day 10**
Carry Your Own Weather	Inspire Trust	Model Work/Life Balance	Place the Right People in the Right Roles	Make Time for Relationships
Day 11	**Day 12**	**Day 13**	**Day 14**	**Day 15**
Check Your Paradigms	Lead Difficult Conversations	Talk Straight	Balance Courage and Consideration	Show Loyalty
Day 16	**Day 17**	**Day 18**	**Day 19**	**Day 20**
Make It Safe to Tell the Truth	Right Wrongs	Coach Continuously	Protect Your Team Against Urgencies	Hold Regular 1-on-1s
Day 21	**Day 22**	**Day 23**	**Day 24**	**Day 25**
Allow Others to Be Smart	Create Vision	Identify the Wildly Important Goals® (WIGs®)	Align Actions with the Wildly Important Goals	Ensure Your Systems Support Your Mission
Day 26	**Day 27**	**Day 28**	**Day 29**	**Day 30**
Deliver Results	Celebrate Wins	Make High-Value Decisions	Lead Through Change	Get Better

CHALLENGE 13

TALK STRAIGHT

When was the last time you technically told the truth, but left a misleading impression?

Many people have mastered a unique specialty:

- French cooking: Julia Child
- Tennis: Roger Federer
- Magic: David Copperfield
- Talking Straight: Joan Rivers (and me)

That's how practiced I am at this. To quote our CEO, "You don't need an interpreter to understand what Scott is thinking." I'm guessing that wasn't entirely a compliment, but at the same time, this leadership challenge is a bit messy for me. Sometimes an overdone strength can be just as damaging as one that's absent altogether.

It was 2004, and I was halfway into my six-year "reign of terror" (as my then-associates now refer to it) in Chicago. Business was growing and recovering nicely from the 2001 recession. I was still on the left side of my leadership learning curve, and typically taking the proverbial two steps forward and one back. Tensions in the office were palpable. I didn't see it then, but I'm now told I was a classic micromanager and know-it-all jerk— likable at times, but increasingly feared by many. It was a tough role to be in: transforming a division that had been leaderless for nearly two years, with associates either aimless or outright taking advantage of the company. That reality aside, it all came to a surprising head one day.

Although the broader division had about forty associates, the actual office was smaller, about fifteen people, and we worked closely together. I hired nearly every one of them, a very talented group of professionals, and they all liked each other (key words there are *they* and *each other*). Paul Walker was then a junior salesperson but becoming a culture leader on the team. I suspect there must have been a team meeting and Paul was nominated to take on the straight-talk task.

Paul walked into my office one morning and, with flawless delivery, lowered the boom: *"Everyone here hates you, and if something doesn't change, we're all going to quit."*

These are the types of statements that don't leave much open to interpretation. This was uncharacteristic of Paul, as this level of courage and talking straight wasn't (yet) his brand. He was confident but respectful of my position. Paul was more the quiet type who would endure jerks like me and then announce one day he was leaving for another opportunity. He closed the door and we sat for over two hours and talked—transparently and with no limits. We talked about what was happening and why, and we listened to each other. I worked to understand the gravity of my behavior, and Paul worked to understand all of the pressures I was facing from above me.

We both cried. I will never forget it: likely one of the most selfless and generous gifts ever given to me. Paul called out exactly what it was like to work with me, drawing upon specific encounters and conversations. He clearly boxed me in, so I understood the magnitude of the pain I was causing. He also afforded me the chance to share my own challenges—what it was like sitting on my side of the desk each day; the pressures I was under; some of the issues I was facing. It was a very healing and introspective conversation.

> NOT EVERY CULTURE VALUES STRAIGHT TALK. AS A LEADER, IT'S YOUR JUDGMENT TO UNDERSTAND YOUR LATITUDE. STRAIGHT TALK CAN BE DELIVERED IN RESPECTFUL AND HONORABLE WAYS WITHOUT EVER DIMINISHING SOMEONE'S REPUTATION.

I think things got incrementally better. I remained the leader for about three more years, mentoring Paul as my eventual successor. I believe that the straight talk I have consistently used and modeled for others, while not always pleasant to hear, has been a catalyst for really helping them become better. I *know* the straight talk I received from Paul that day certainly did it for me.

Not every culture values straight talk. As a leader, it's your judgment to understand your latitude. Straight talk can be delivered in respectful and honorable ways without ever diminishing someone's reputation.

So, what's the opposite of straight talk? Posturing, positioning, spinning, or technically telling the truth but leaving the wrong impression.

Failing to talk straight is a leadership slippery slope, as the *real* truth is bound to show up sooner or later. Then a leader is forced to either out-and-out lie, or admit they were deliberately leaving a false impression. Either way, that leader's credibility is about to get flushed down a porcelain slippery slope of its own.

But what about *well-intentioned* spinning? You know, the little lies that spare the feelings of others or save them from psychological harm? Researchers have found that lying to "help" another person is almost always perceived to be good, while lying that had no effect on the other person or that harmed someone is perceived to be wrong.

So, what does the skillful leader do? Is it okay to live in the nebulous region between lies and truth so long as your intentions are good? I'm guessing not so much.

Thankfully, Stephen M. R. Covey tackled this philosophically heavy topic in his book *The Speed of Trust*. He characterized talking straight as "honesty in action," expressed as telling the truth and leaving the right impression. He wrote that effective leaders use straight talk that is "tempered by skill, tact, and good judgment."

Organizational culture typically flows from the top. Do you and your peer leaders communicate clearly? Do you call things by their right names? It turns out that words matter. Like, really, really matter. As leaders, our ability to talk straight comes down to using clear, accurate, and simple language to ensure that what is said is what is heard and, perhaps most important, what is being heard is being understood. Leaders who talk straight:

- Call things by their right names using common, plain language.

- Don't spin or position for the sake of posturing.

- Tell the truth in diplomatic yet clear language.

- Don't try to sound more intelligent than they are.

Leaders who talk straight leave their listeners clear about the intended message because there was nothing added to distract or confuse. No extra slides. No long effusive speeches. No multisyllable words to impress or intimidate. They don't leave room for misinterpretation or guessing. They stay as far from spin as possible.

FROM MESS TO SUCCESS:
TALK STRAIGHT

- Think about where or with whom you tend to "spin" or even withhold the truth.

- Identify possible reasons you are avoiding straight talk.

  1. Do you talk differently with your leader than you do your peers?
  2. Do certain types of colleagues somehow encourage or discourage your propensity to talk straight? Why?

- Next time you notice yourself "spinning," pause, then find a more accurate and tempered way to tell the whole truth.

Day 1	Day 2	Day 3	Day 4	Day 5
Demonstrate Humility	Think Abundantly	Listen First	Declare Your Intent	Make and Keep Commitments
Day 6	**Day 7**	**Day 8**	**Day 9**	**Day 10**
Carry Your Own Weather	Inspire Trust	Model Work/Life Balance	Place the Right People in the Right Roles	Make Time for Relationships
Day 11	**Day 12**	**Day 13**	**Day 14**	**Day 15**
Check Your Paradigms	Lead Difficult Conversations	Talk Straight	Balance Courage and Consideration	Show Loyalty
Day 16	**Day 17**	**Day 18**	**Day 19**	**Day 20**
Make It Safe to Tell the Truth	Right Wrongs	Coach Continuously	Protect Your Team Against Urgencies	Hold Regular 1-on-1s
Day 21	**Day 22**	**Day 23**	**Day 24**	**Day 25**
Allow Others to Be Smart	Create Vision	Identify the Wildly Important Goals® (WIGs®)	Align Actions with the Wildly Important Goals	Ensure Your Systems Support Your Mission
Day 26	**Day 27**	**Day 28**	**Day 29**	**Day 30**
Deliver Results	Celebrate Wins	Make High-Value Decisions	Lead Through Change	Get Better

CHALLENGE 14

BALANCE COURAGE AND CONSIDERATION

Do your wins come at the expense of others? Or
do you allow others to win at your expense?

Most of the thirty leadership challenges in this book don't come naturally to me (and I've been in the leadership-development industry for nearly my entire career). I've had to learn them the hard way, often through failure, public rebuke, or outright humiliation. And this one is no exception.

HOW DO LEADERS FIND THIS BALANCE WHILE ACCOMMODATING THE DIVERSE NEEDS, PREFERENCES, AND TRAITS OF OUR TEAM MEMBERS? BY DEMONSTRATING COURAGE IN SHARING OPINIONS, TACTFULLY CALLING OUT MISTAKES (INCLUDING OUR OWN), AND DIPLOMATICALLY CHALLENGING ONE'S DIRECTION WHILE SIMULTANEOUSLY ACCOUNTING FOR PEOPLE'S FEELINGS, INSECURITIES, AND CULTURAL NORMS.

The best leaders assess their balance of courage and consideration intentionally and repeatedly. Courage often means telling it like it is, calling things out, stepping up to difficult conversations, and addressing tough issues. It also sometimes means saying *nothing*. When overdone, it can take the form of bullying, being overly brash and undiplomatic, or lacking empathy. Consideration often means showing kindness, being polite, and assuming the best in others. Too much consideration can become avoidance, capitulation, neglect, and disenfranchisement.

Most of us have a natural tendency to one or the other—how, where, and even when you were raised will influence your style. I've shared on the podcast I host that, in my late teens, a new neighbor moved in across the street. I viewed her as the epitome of success: she'd bought a nice home, had two sports cars, owned a thriving business, and employed a nanny. I interpreted her loud, abrupt, and take-charge style as the secret to her success. I'm comfortable admitting that I quickly adopted it. Almost overnight, I went from being rather passive and easily bullied, to being fairly assertive. (My wife would gently correct me and say, "aggressive.")

This high-courage style worked fine in school and at my various hourly jobs. But when I entered the professional workforce, I had so neglected the consideration aspect, that I was constantly being reprimanded, until finally being "exited" from my first professional role. I had plenty of courage to strike my own path and do things my way, but I lacked the consideration to collaborate with others. To get back on track, I had to compromise, adapt to new organizational cultures, learn the value of diplomacy, and become more consciously considerate of others.

Interestingly, even if you've struck a good balance personally, some organizational cultures, teams, or roles may require more courage or consideration than you're used to. Every culture has its own equilibrium. Some value brasher, more outspoken styles, while others prefer a hold-your-tongue approach to avoid conflict. For example, when your leader announces that Casual Fridays have been canceled, does your team passionately argue against it, or do they put their heads down and silently lament the new reality? In some cultures, it may require a divining rod to uncover the right balance.

Over my career, some have called me the proverbial bull in a china shop. The "china shop" is in fact the FranklinCovey organization, where the culture has historically erred on the high side of consideration. It has generally had a careful, polite, and nonconfrontational culture—a reflection of Utah, where it is headquartered (not altogether a bad thing). Our "conservative" ways have been a strong asset driving our growth, our success with clients, and our well-earned credibility over thirty-five years. But this high-consideration culture can make it difficult for people with more courageous styles to assimilate. Like, for example, me.

This particular "bull" has what many would call an "East Coast personality." In other words, a predilection for high courage. As mentioned, I deliberately cultivated that style, but certainly there is some truth that we East Coasters have a tell-it-like-it-is, call-it-as-we-see-it kind of reputation. (Obviously, not everyone from a particular region or culture is the same, but indulge this generalization for a moment.) Juxtapose that with another sweeping generalization some might call "Utah-nice" and you can see the impending bull vs. china-shop collision.

When I moved from the East Coast to Utah, I had to calibrate my balance and learn a new language to decode unknown (to me) verbal, body-language, and cultural nuances. When someone at work said, "Scott, you're so funny," they were neither laughing nor finding me funny. This was Utah-speak for, "Scott, you're rather offensive, and we don't talk that way here." I bet if I had moved to New Jersey instead of the Wasatch Mountains, they would have seen me as mildly entertaining and somewhat bland.

How do leaders find this balance while accommodating the diverse needs, preferences, and traits of our team members? By demonstrating

...WITHOUT CONSCIOUSLY STRIKING THE RIGHT BALANCE BETWEEN COURAGE AND CONSIDERATION, OUR RESULTS AND RELATIONSHIPS WILL SUFFER. BEING AWARE OF YOUR IMBALANCE IS THE FIRST STEP TO BRINGING BALANCE BACK.

courage in sharing opinions, tactfully calling out mistakes (including our own), and diplomatically challenging one's direction while simultaneously accounting for people's feelings, insecurities, and cultural norms. Geographical and organizational cultures do affect the courage/consideration balance, but principled leaders can thrive anywhere because most people want to hear truth when it's respectfully presented. Effective leaders excel at managing their emotions while achieving high levels of trust. They are regarded as level-headed, diplomatic, and trustworthy.

Many cultural misalignments and interpersonal conflicts are caused by otherwise very competent and well-intended leaders who can't find the right balance between courage and consideration. I'm probably not alone in having to learn this the hard way. Perhaps we've adopted our parents' styles, tried to emulate a politician or world figure we've admired from afar, or spent too much time thinking about the single new neighbor and her two sports cars. But without consciously striking the right balance between courage and consideration, our results and relationships will suffer. Being aware of your imbalance is the first step to bringing balance back.

FROM MESS TO SUCCESS:
BALANCE COURAGE AND CONSIDERATION

- Find a colleague whom you trust. Ask for specific examples of when they've seen you out of balance. Ask:

    1. When do you feel I'm being overly nice or too considerate?
    2. When have you seen me be too tough, abrasive, or "in your face" with others?

- Be mindful of triggers that may push you to overdoing consideration or courage. These could be specific people, situations, or topics.

- Have the courage to ask *and* act.

Day 1 Demonstrate Humility	**Day 2** Think Abundantly	**Day 3** Listen First	**Day 4** Declare Your Intent	**Day 5** Make and Keep Commitments
Day 6 Carry Your Own Weather	**Day 7** Inspire Trust	**Day 8** Model Work/Life Balance	**Day 9** Place the Right People in the Right Roles	**Day 10** Make Time for Relationships
Day 11 Check Your Paradigms	**Day 12** Lead Difficult Conversations	**Day 13** Talk Straight	**Day 14** Balance Courage and Consideration	**Day 15** Show Loyalty
Day 16 Make It Safe to Tell the Truth	**Day 17** Right Wrongs	**Day 18** Coach Continuously	**Day 19** Protect Your Team Against Urgencies	**Day 20** Hold Regular 1-on-1s
Day 21 Allow Others to Be Smart	**Day 22** Create Vision	**Day 23** Identify the Wildly Important Goals® (WIGs®)	**Day 24** Align Actions with the Wildly Important Goals	**Day 25** Ensure Your Systems Support Your Mission
Day 26 Deliver Results	**Day 27** Celebrate Wins	**Day 28** Make High-Value Decisions	**Day 29** Lead Through Change	**Day 30** Get Better

CHALLENGE 15

SHOW LOYALTY

When was the last time you gossiped or disparaged someone behind their back?

Is it human nature to gossip? I fear so.

I don't think I knew gossiping was inherently toxic until I was twenty-seven, the year I joined FranklinCovey. In every setting I'd ever been in, gossiping was the norm: school, church, Boy Scouts, part-time jobs, clubs, the local recreation center, my neighborhood, dinner and holiday parties, political campaigns—all of it was grounded in gossip. It was normal behavior in everyone I'd ever met, everywhere. It didn't mean these people were bad; they were just talking about each other. Gossiping seemed no different from driving 5 miles over the highway speed limit—everyone admitted to doing it (and the rest were probably lying).

> BOB WHITMAN, OUR CEO, MODELS LOYALTY FROM THE TOP OF OUR ORGANIZATION. BOB DOES NOT GOSSIP, NOR DOES HE TOLERATE IT FROM OTHERS. IT'S A "NO DEAL" FOR HIM. HE DOESN'T SHAME ANYONE INTO COMPLIANCE; INSTEAD HE MODELS WHAT HE WANTS TO SEE IN OTHERS...BOB UNDERSTANDS THAT GOSSIP ISN'T ALWAYS OVERT: SOMETIMES, SPEAKING ON ANOTHER'S BEHALF ALLOWS SMALL BIASES, ERRORS IN JUDGEMENT, OR MISREPRESENTATIONS TO SLIP IN. BELIEVE ME, WHEN THAT'S THE LEVEL OF GOSSIPING THE CEO DOESN'T ALLOW, ANYTHING IN THE MUD-SLINGING CATEGORY DOESN'T STAND A CHANCE.

Back in the '90s, there was a popular and hilarious comedy show called *In Living Color.* One of the characters, played by Kim Wayans, was a nosy neighbor named Benita Butrell. Her signature line was, "But I ain't one to gossip, so you ain't heard that from me!" She would then promptly sell out anyone and everyone with hilariously juicy tidbits from their personal lives: It was funny as much for her genius and flawless delivery as it was for mocking everyday life. We all have a bit of Benita Butrell in us.

I didn't consciously stop gossiping until I joined Covey Leadership Center (a precursor to FranklinCovey), which introduced me to the concept of "being loyal to the absent." Dr. Covey said, "When you defend those who are absent, you retain the trust of those present." This saying shocked me into understanding the pervasive cultural damage gossip inflicts inside organizations. Showing loyalty to others is a simple but profound leadership competency.

Stephen M. R. Covey deemed this principle so vital that he included it as one of his 13 Behaviors® of High-Trust Leaders. My own hard-learned lesson around showing loyalty occurred in 2001. I had just been promoted to the managing director of a fifteen-state region based in Chicago. Concurrently, as a new managing director, I sat on the president's leadership team, where I was privy to sensitive strategic information about company moves and personnel issues. Embarrassingly, I still hadn't developed the level of maturity to keep confidences and engaged in light gossip here and there. (Important disclaimer: I was not sharing insider information or corporate trade secrets. It was more like, "Hey, I think Sally's getting the axe next weekend." Petty, I know.)

Sometime later, I found the company president in my office for a scheduled meeting. We sat across from each other in two red leather chairs—chairs I distinctly remember as having gold rivets and brown legs; chairs that are, forever, viscerally burned into my memory, as they relate to the context of what I was about to hear. The president looked me in the eye and said, "Scott, you're standing at a gas station and you're holding a match."

Apparently, my small acts of verbal disloyalty had found their way to his ears. What followed was a high-courage conversation where he shared his frustration at my inability to keep confidences and be loyal to him. If you can imagine me pressing myself into that soft leather chair and wanting to disappear, you wouldn't be far from the truth.

Oh, the pain I would have saved myself and those around me in those first years, had I adopted this principle into my life. But because of this thoughtful leader's straight talk and willingness to coach me, I made an almost immediate 180-degree turn. Since then, I've become a named executive officer with access to highly privileged information. I fully abide by all of those protocols. Have I fully stopped gossiping? Sadly, no. But I've certainly improved.

Bob Whitman, our CEO, models loyalty from the top of our organization. Bob does not gossip, nor does he tolerate it from others. It's a "no deal" for him. He doesn't shame anyone into compliance; instead he models what he wants to see in others. When one of us misses our "do not miss" weekly meeting (it happens mainly when we're out working with clients), one of the other executive team members sometimes starts to represent the absent person's point of view. Bob will never let this happen, however. He will, without fail, suspend the discussion until the missing team member can represent his or her own position, behavior, or decision. Bob understands that gossip isn't always overt: sometimes, speaking on another's behalf allows small biases, errors in judgement, or misrepresentations to slip in. Believe me, when that's the level of gossiping the CEO doesn't allow, anything in the mud-slinging category doesn't stand a chance.

Consider these recommendations for showing loyalty to others:

- Live by the Platinum Rule. A wise friend of mine once told me that, beyond treating people how *you'd* like to be treated (the Golden Rule), treat them how *they'd* like to be treated (the Platinum Rule).

- When someone is absent, speak about them as if they were actually standing there right beside you. Visualizing the person being present will dramatically change how you talk about them.

- Assume your email will be forwarded to the person you're writing about. When composing an email about another person, write as if you know the person will eventually read it. Also, the use of "bcc:" is cowardly and disloyal, and something to avoid nearly all of the time.

- Assume good intent. Human beings are often conditioned to assume others have bad intentions. Stop and reflect on someone's actions with the assumption they had good intentions.

- Presume every private conversation is confidential unless/until you can verify that it's not.

Once the value of loyalty permeates your company culture, you'll wonder how you ever functioned without it.

FROM MESS TO SUCCESS:
SHOW LOYALTY

- Think back to a time when someone was disloyal to you. What was the impact?

- When did you last fail to show loyalty? Why? What would you do differently?

- If a conversation misrepresents someone who is absent, say, "I'll reserve judgment until I speak to them directly."

- If you find you're representing another's point of view, consider waiting until that person can speak for himself or herself.

- The next time you receive a compliment for your team's work, share the credit instead of taking it for yourself.

Day 1	Day 2	Day 3	Day 4	Day 5
Demonstrate Humility	Think Abundantly	Listen First	Declare Your Intent	Make and Keep Commitments
Day 6	**Day 7**	**Day 8**	**Day 9**	**Day 10**
Carry Your Own Weather	Inspire Trust	Model Work/Life Balance	Place the Right People in the Right Roles	Make Time for Relationships
Day 11	**Day 12**	**Day 13**	**Day 14**	**Day 15**
Check Your Paradigms	Lead Difficult Conversations	Talk Straight	Balance Courage and Consideration	Show Loyalty
Day 16	**Day 17**	**Day 18**	**Day 19**	**Day 20**
Make It Safe to Tell the Truth	Right Wrongs	Coach Continuously	Protect Your Team Against Urgencies	Hold Regular 1-on-1s
Day 21	**Day 22**	**Day 23**	**Day 24**	**Day 25**
Allow Others to Be Smart	Create Vision	Identify the Wildly Important Goals® (WIGs®)	Align Actions with the Wildly Important Goals	Ensure Your Systems Support Your Mission
Day 26	**Day 27**	**Day 28**	**Day 29**	**Day 30**
Deliver Results	Celebrate Wins	Make High-Value Decisions	Lead Through Change	Get Better

CHALLENGE 16

MAKE IT SAFE TO TELL THE TRUTH

Are your people as forthcoming with bad news and negative feedback as they are with good news and positive feedback?

I've long believed feedback is more the responsibility of the receiver than the giver. And when I say more, I mean *much* more. I believe humans are inherently cowardly when communicating. I suspect we can trace some of it back to our childhood and well-meaning advice from adults:

- "If you don't have anything nice to say, don't say anything at all."

- "Remember, never say anything you wouldn't want said about yourself."

- "You have two ears and one mouth, so use them proportionately."

- "People who live in glass houses shouldn't throw stones."

No wonder we can get too focused on showing respect, being courteous, or demonstrating restraint. And because most of us don't say what we're thinking, the other person assumes everything is A-okay (no problems here!). But the reality is that, in most professional settings, we can make big improvements in our emotional maturity, interpersonal skills, and self-awareness—if someone gives us feedback on them.

> I'VE LONG BELIEVED FEEDBACK IS MORE THE RESPONSIBILITY OF THE RECEIVER THAN THE GIVER. AND WHEN I SAY MORE, I MEAN MUCH MORE. I BELIEVE HUMANS ARE INHERENTLY COWARDLY WHEN COMMUNICATING.

We've all seen firsthand what happens when people don't feel safe to tell the truth. Remember when the CEO made a ninety-minute, 240-slide speech at the annual company kickoff meeting? You know, the one that should have been twenty minutes long with only a handful of slides? Remember what happened afterward? The shower of accolades punctuated by "Great job!" "You were excellent!" and "Great speech, boss!" Meanwhile, you were thinking: *That totally sucked.* And all the texting around the room confirmed the same.

Now put yourself in the place of the CEO. How does *not* hearing the truth serve you? Maybe you think because the vast majority of the audience had nothing to say, that you nailed it. But here's what I've noticed over my career: The higher up you get in an organization, the more insulated you are from the truth. By the time you hit the twentieth-floor corner office, feedback will be as thin as the air is rarefied.

This is why I started the challenge by declaring that feedback is the main responsibility of the receiver and not the giver. Thus, the phrase *make it safe to tell the truth* is talking about you, the leader, owning the responsibility to make it safe for others to be truthful. As a leader, you should want to hear the truth for many reasons:

- To really know how others perceive you.

- To understand what it's like to be in a relationship (personal or professional) with you.

- To know your blind spots so you can address them.

- To assess whether your communication skills lift or diminish others.

- To have an accurate view of your performance, brand, and reputation.

- To evaluate what it's like to be a member of your team.

- To gauge how it feels to be on your good or bad side.

- To learn the reality about a business issue early on, so you can address it before it's too hard, too late, or too expensive to solve.

- To ensure the messenger knows you will not make it personal.

WE'VE ALL SEEN FIRSTHAND WHAT HAPPENS WHEN PEOPLE DON'T FEEL SAFE TO TELL THE TRUTH. REMEMBER WHEN THE CEO MADE A NINETY-MINUTE, 240-SLIDE SPEECH AT THE ANNUAL COMPANY KICKOFF MEETING? YOU KNOW, THE ONE THAT SHOULD HAVE BEEN TWENTY MINUTES LONG WITH ONLY A HANDFUL OF SLIDES? REMEMBER WHAT HAPPENED AFTERWARD? THE SHOWER OF ACCOLADES PUNCTUATED BY "GREAT JOB!", "YOU WERE EXCELLENT!" AND "GREAT SPEECH, BOSS!" MEANWHILE YOU WERE THINKING: THAT SUCKED.

Researchers have found that humans are wired to lie. Absent safety, our old lizard brains ratchet up our sense of risk. It's been my lifelong experience that, even if I *beg* people to tell me the truth about how they perceive me, they will still obfuscate and say something like, "You're great, Scott. And I'm great. Everything is great." (Unless they truly hate me, then watch out. I'll save those examples for a future book, likely titled *150 Different Ways I've Been Told to Go to Hell*.)

Here's how to help make it safe for others to be truthful in your presence:

- Show sincerity in wanting to know their truth. (I say *their* because not everyone's version is accurate, complete, or helpful.)

- Build their confidence that there is zero downside to speaking up (no retribution, punishment, or risk).

- Convey that you respect their point of view and will be vulnerable (especially to associates junior to you).

- Prove through continued experience that you won't dispute or challenge their position, defend your behavior, or dismiss their feedback out of hand.

- Perhaps most important, show through your new behavior that you value their risk-taking enough to improve.

- Don't lure someone to the "safe" side of the pool and then push their head below the surface.

- Show how you valued others who provided you with feedback, and that there was only an upside in them doing so.

- Carefully consider the physical setting. Don't invite someone into your office and sit behind your massive desk and gargoyle-themed garniture expecting courage. Find neutral ground to show you're not above them or anything they have to say.

- Take notes and ask for clarification.

- Genuinely ask for specific examples.

- Encourage them to give feedback.

- Do not defend or refute.

Sometimes emailing and asking for feedback can be the best vehicle for truth-telling. Most people will be more courageous in an email than face-to-face, especially with the boss. You might ask them to ponder a question over several days and then send their thoughts back electronically. You always have the option for a face-to-face meeting if you need additional context.

Remember, only *you* can create the conditions where lying isn't rewarded and telling the truth is safe and even championed.

FROM MESS TO SUCCESS:
MAKE IT SAFE
TO TELL THE TRUTH

- Consider what you're doing to encourage or discourage others from sharing with you their truth about you.

- Assess your current organization or team. Is lying or spinning rewarded? Is truth-telling unsafe?

- Communicate that mistakes are inevitable and candid feedback is welcome.

- Show that you value feedback by changing your behavior and thanking the giver.

- Above all, when someone does take the risk to provide feedback, don't dismiss it, disregard it, or defend yourself. Listen, show appreciation, then discern on your own whether it's worthy of acting on. Some feedback will be more about the person offering it than about you.

Day 1	Day 2	Day 3	Day 4	Day 5
Demonstrate Humility	Think Abundantly	Listen First	Declare Your Intent	Make and Keep Commitments
Day 6	Day 7	Day 8	Day 9	Day 10
Carry Your Own Weather	Inspire Trust	Model Work/Life Balance	Place the Right People in the Right Roles	Make Time for Relationships
Day 11	Day 12	Day 13	Day 14	Day 15
Check Your Paradigms	Lead Difficult Conversations	Talk Straight	Balance Courage and Consideration	Show Loyalty
Day 16	Day 17	Day 18	Day 19	Day 20
Make It Safe to Tell the Truth	Right Wrongs	Coach Continuously	Protect Your Team Against Urgencies	Hold Regular 1-on-1s
Day 21	Day 22	Day 23	Day 24	Day 25
Allow Others to Be Smart	Create Vision	Identify the Wildly Important Goals® (WIGs®)	Align Actions with the Wildly Important Goals	Ensure Your Systems Support Your Mission
Day 26	Day 27	Day 28	Day 29	Day 30
Deliver Results	Celebrate Wins	Make High-Value Decisions	Lead Through Change	Get Better

CHALLENGE 17

RIGHT WRONGS

When you break a promise, is your first
instinct to defend yourself, rationalize,
minimize, or ignore it altogether?

I recently interviewed the famed author and former editor of the *Harvard Business Review,* **Karen Dillon.** Besides writing several of her own books, she's coauthored three with Harvard Professor Clayton Christensen. My favorite is *How Will You Measure Your Life?* This ingenious tome is a must-add to your reading list. The authors brilliantly apply innovative business principles to our personal lives.

I found it compelling, thought-provoking, and actionable. For example, the authors define humility as being grounded in confidence. Humble people are secure in their self-esteem and their capabilities. There's no need for hubris, puffery, or defensiveness. They show their humility through their confidence. Deep, huh?

...MY MENTOR CHUCK FARNSWORTH AND AN EMPOWERING CONCEPT HE TERMED "PRE-FORGIVENESS." ESSENTIALLY, IT MEANS: YOU'RE PRE-FORGIVEN. YOU WILL MAKE MISTAKES. IT'S PART OF EACH OF OUR JOURNEYS. IF WE LIVE IN FEAR OF MAKING A MISSTEP, WE WON'T PLACE ANY BETS, TAKE ANY RISKS, OR STRETCH OUR SKILLS.

In my experience, humble (i.e., confident) people find it remarkably easy to right wrongs, especially by apologizing to others. They quickly repair any damage caused by their actions or words. I suspect it's almost effortless for them, because they feel no need to defend or contextualize. Being wrong or vulnerable doesn't make them weaker. Quite the opposite.

But that's not the way the world sees it. And in the fledgling days of my career, it wasn't the point of view I started with either. Just so you know, I'm the guy who purchased "I'm Sorry" cards *in bulk.* There are psychological incentives for *not* apologizing. According to researchers, refusing to apologize can make you feel more empowered and in control. Ironically, these feelings often drive an even higher sense of self-worth and personal integrity. I bought into that—hook, line, and sinker.

Fast-forward a few years to my mentor Chuck Farnsworth and an empowering concept he termed "pre-forgiveness." Essentially, it means: *You're pre-forgiven. You will make mistakes. It's part of each of our journeys. If we live in fear of making a misstep, we won't place any bets, take any risks, or stretch our skills.*

I felt completely empowered to be working for him. And what leader wouldn't want a team who felt that way? Is it any mystery that his team had some of the lowest turnover in the organization? Chuck decided to pre-forgive in his mind (and yes, heart), and he communicated it to his team. If you want to reduce the time and effort it takes to right wrongs, announce that you've pre-forgiven any missteps, hurtful remarks, insensitive communications, or errors in judgment that might occur. That doesn't mean people get a free pass for bad behavior, but rather you acknowledge that everyone falls short, and it's okay.

When righting wrongs, it's remarkably disarming to take full responsibility. I'm amazed at the speed with which the aggrieved person lets go of their pent-up anger or resentment. Nothing neutralizes anger more than a sincere, excuse-free apology and an action to correct the situation. Consider some version of the following when you find yourself having wronged someone:

"I want to tell you something very important. I'm truly sorry for the way I behaved. I was wrong. I own it. I'm sorry. I hope you can forgive me, and I intend to make a sincere effort to ensure I don't ever do that to you again or to anyone else. I have learned a hard and valuable lesson, sadly at your expense, and I want you to know how seriously I am taking it. Furthermore, I intend to take [fill in the blank] action to make it right between us. Is that something you would value, or do you have a better suggestion I should consider?"

The best leaders know how to right wrongs. If you start out by saying, "Mistakes were made" or "My bad," you've gone off the track. Righting wrongs starts from a place of humility and is communicated through personal responsibility. As with most acts of leadership, it's easier for us authors to offer some uplifting words than for you to actually go back and implement it with people in your life. Like peppermint schnapps on New Year's Eve: start small and work your way up.

FROM MESS TO SUCCESS:
RIGHT WRONGS

- Consider instituting a pre-forgiveness culture with your team. Talk with each other about what that really means and come to some agreements about the positive and negative implications.

- If you've violated an expectation or broken a promise, acknowledge it. Resist the urge to rationalize.

- Take full responsibility by offering an unconditional apology, then take action to right the wrong. An excuse-laden apology is only remembered for the excuse, not the apology.

- Recognize that if you have to apologize often, there may be other issues to address. Also remember the adage "If you're not pissing someone off, you're probably not accomplishing anything." Find the balance between them.

Day 1	Day 2	Day 3	Day 4	Day 5
Demonstrate Humility	Think Abundantly	Listen First	Declare Your Intent	Make and Keep Commitments
Day 6	**Day 7**	**Day 8**	**Day 9**	**Day 10**
Carry Your Own Weather	Inspire Trust	Model Work/Life Balance	Place the Right People in the Right Roles	Make Time for Relationships
Day 11	**Day 12**	**Day 13**	**Day 14**	**Day 15**
Check Your Paradigms	Lead Difficult Conversations	Talk Straight	Balance Courage and Consideration	Show Loyalty
Day 16	**Day 17**	**Day 18**	**Day 19**	**Day 20**
Make It Safe to Tell the Truth	Right Wrongs	Coach Continuously	Protect Your Team Against Urgencies	Hold Regular 1-on-1s
Day 21	**Day 22**	**Day 23**	**Day 24**	**Day 25**
Allow Others to Be Smart	Create Vision	Identify the Wildly Important Goals® (WIGs®)	Align Actions with the Wildly Important Goals	Ensure Your Systems Support Your Mission
Day 26	**Day 27**	**Day 28**	**Day 29**	**Day 30**
Deliver Results	Celebrate Wins	Make High-Value Decisions	Lead Through Change	Get Better

CHALLENGE 18

COACH CONTINUOUSLY

Do you see every interaction with team
members as an opportunity to build
confidence and develop potential?

Here's what the opposite of "Coach Continuously" looks like: You have your annual performance appraisal scheduled on your calendar. It's two weeks out, but it's both exciting and nerve-wracking. You're certain your boss will spend most of it praising you and recognizing the significant value you've brought to the team, department, division, and company. You could improve in some areas, sure, but that's nothing compared to the coronation headed your way.

When Appraisal Day comes, you take your seat, both a little nervous and optimistic. Then you pick up on some subtle clues that things aren't about to go the way you thought:

- There appears to be a box of Kleenex recently placed on *your* side of the desk.

- And it's next to a copy of *You and the Underperforming Employee*.

- The motivational poster about "Teamwork!" has been replaced with one that reads, "The Long Road to Improvement."

Then it happens. Your boss lays out all your inadequacies and failures with the precision of a prosecutor making an opening statement. Pages of notes (i.e., "documentation") detail the point-by-point case as you sit stunned at the direction the meeting has taken. You can't even hear what your boss is saying because you're so incredulous at the "evidence" they're bringing up from four months ago, nine months ago, staff meetings, and projects you barely remember.

IN HER BOOK ON DEATH AND DYING, ELISABETH KUBLER-ROSS FAMOUSLY OUTLINED FIVE STAGES OF GRIEF: DENIAL, ANGER, BARGAINING, DEPRESSION, AND ACCEPTANCE. THERE ARE SOME EERIE SIMILARITIES BETWEEN A SUDDEN DEATH AND AN AMBUSH PERFORMANCE REVIEW.

It's finally over after you've signed your performance plan. (It's feeling like a divorce at this point, with your spouse keeping the kids, house, your vintage car from high school, the dog, and pretty much everything else save the credit-card debt.) You leave feeling eviscerated. Not because your boss was mean, rude, or abrupt, but because you're so taken aback. Ambushed, even. You can't believe what just happened and think about finding another job.

In her book *On Death and Dying*, Elisabeth Kubler-Ross famously outlined five stages of grief: denial, anger, bargaining, depression, and acceptance. There are some eerie similarities between a sudden death and an ambush performance review. Appraisal conversations like the one I just illustrated can destroy people's self-esteem and self-confidence. Worse, they can permanently degrade someone's self-worth.

Fortunately, increasingly rare are the days of the annual, mandated performance appraisal, where you're force-ranked against your colleagues to watch the lowest fed to the lions and the precious bonus pool allocated to the lucky few at the top. Yet, a few persist, and leaders find a way to hide behind the processes of formal, sit-down appraisals. As a result, they often end up ensnaring their subordinates with a host of pent-up frustrations, perceived slights, or long-brewing performance issues. Many such concerns, had they been addressed in real time, could have been dealt with and helped the person's career flourish instead of languish.

The antidote to all of this is the often-neglected role of the leader as a coach. And coaching continuously requires a lot of engagement. First, you have to inherently *want* to lift others up, not just by affirming what they're doing right, but also by addressing what's wrong, slightly off, or even unacceptable. It takes a mindset shift, courage, diplomacy, practice, and repetition. You'll recognize that many of the challenges you've already read about will be useful in developing your coaching skills, including: "Talk Straight," "Lead Difficult Conversations," "Balance Courage and Consideration," and others.

An entire industry is dedicated to coaching: books, training, university programs, organizations, and certifications. FranklinCovey has its own coaching practice, arguably the best in the industry, committed to executive coaching. Much of the advice I'm about to offer aligns with what experts or credentialed coaches will tell you. But this is coaching as I've experienced it—imperfect and often messy, but real, relevant, and replicable. Here are several behaviors that have benefited me greatly when I've been coached:

- Be aware of what's happening with the team you lead. Who's struggling and why? Are they properly trained? aligned? delivering solid results, but perhaps working on the wrong initiatives? Have you clarified what success looks like? Are deliverables clear and goals translated into actions and daily behaviors? These previous points are mainly your responsibility.

- Have a "check in" versus a "check on" process. This is especially true if you're leading a virtual team and can't see what's going on up close. Be Proactive so you know if someone needs help before it's too late.

- Recognize the different ways team members want and need coaching. Some people shut down and are embarrassed if called out in public, while others couldn't care less and have a bring-it-on personality. Calibrate your style to their unique needs.

- Balance your critical feedback with specific reinforcing praise. Coaching continuously isn't just about what's going wrong. It's a great chance to let people know what's working, what to double down on, and what to pull back from.

- Ask how you can help. Be present and aware. When you're coaching, give the other person the benefit of your full attention.

- Ensure that everyone has the resources and tools to complete their work and help others.

- Add "coaching" to your daily task list. Use the prompt to remind you to look for authentic chances to coach.

To quote my friend Paul Walker, "Telling reinforces dependency; coaching develops capability."

FROM MESS TO SUCCESS:
COACH CONTINUOUSLY

- Extend real-time coaching beyond your 1-on-1s and formal performance reviews.

- Implement at least one of the coaching best practices with a team member during the upcoming week.

- Review your interactions. How much telling did you do versus coaching? Did your team member leave demoralized, or with a "path to improve" and a time frame to revisit?

- Did you balance your time validating, inspiring, and recognizing with challenging and course-correcting?

- Think about those leaders who are the best coaches in your organization. Discuss their strategy and process with them.

Day 1	Day 2	Day 3	Day 4	Day 5
Demonstrate Humility	Think Abundantly	Listen First	Declare Your Intent	Make and Keep Commitments
Day 6	**Day 7**	**Day 8**	**Day 9**	**Day 10**
Carry Your Own Weather	Inspire Trust	Model Work/Life Balance	Place the Right People in the Right Roles	Make Time for Relationships
Day 11	**Day 12**	**Day 13**	**Day 14**	**Day 15**
Check Your Paradigms	Lead Difficult Conversations	Talk Straight	Balance Courage and Consideration	Show Loyalty
Day 16	**Day 17**	**Day 18**	**Day 19**	**Day 20**
Make It Safe to Tell the Truth	Right Wrongs	Coach Continuously	Protect Your Team Against Urgencies	Hold Regular 1-on-1s
Day 21	**Day 22**	**Day 23**	**Day 24**	**Day 25**
Allow Others to Be Smart	Create Vision	Identify the Wildly Important Goals® (WIGs®)	Align Actions with the Wildly Important Goals	Ensure Your Systems Support Your Mission
Day 26	**Day 27**	**Day 28**	**Day 29**	**Day 30**
Deliver Results	Celebrate Wins	Make High-Value Decisions	Lead Through Change	Get Better

CHALLENGE 19

PROTECT YOUR TEAM AGAINST URGENCIES

How will you find the courage to keep your team focused on what is most important, including saying no to some of your own best ideas?

I love a good urgency. And if one doesn't exist, I've been known to create one to satisfy my need to feel relevant. It brings to mind the phenomenon known as either a back-burn or "firefighter arson"—a rare scenario where a firefighter intentionally starts a fire so they can be the hero by arriving first and putting it out. It's unconscionable. And while I can't relate to the actual act of arson in any way, I do find a similarity to my own validation when putting out metaphorical organizational fires. Truth be told, I don't intentionally create fires; but the fact is, I do love fighting them (and the credit that comes from it).

CHANCES ARE YOU'VE SEEN A LEADER GATHER THE TEAM TO PRAISE SOMEONE. AND I BET THE PRAISE WAS FOCUSED MORE ON FIRE FIGHTING THAN FIRE PREVENTION. THE RECOGNITIONS I'VE SEEN (AND ADMITTEDLY, HAVE CALLED OUT MYSELF) ARE USUALLY A HEROIC, LAST-MINUTE EFFORT TO SOLVE A PROBLEM, FIX A MISTAKE, OR RECOVER FROM A CUSTOMER-SERVICE ERROR.

Much of my career has been fueled by this heroic tendency: rushing in to help an executive fix a problem or executing a last-minute idea, both of which are exhilarating to me. I've also been known to offer up an intoxicatingly creative solution, sell it to the C-suite, then marshal my team of thirty around the urgently identified must-do project. Not that being nimble, responsive, proactive, and creative aren't important. These are superb talents to demonstrate in any organization. But when they tip the scale and become your go-to strengths as you constantly put your team through fire drills, it's just not sustainable. Your credibility suffers. Your people grow weary, and you eventually flame out. Your next job can't be in a well-run, focused, and disciplined organization—to be honest, they don't need you. You'll have to search for a company that's in constant chaos and thus will value your firefighting prowess.

I wasn't adept at protecting my team against urgencies until I read FranklinCovey's own time-management book *The 5 Choices: The Path to Extraordinary Productivity* (just proving the adage that the shoemaker's children have no shoes). If you're a corporate adrenaline junkie like me, urgencies can be a tempting distraction. I still feel the tug; it brings me instant validation and gratification. I think the adrenaline high from urgency is invigorating. For a time, anyway. Then it peaks and quickly fatigues people. You're seen as overly tactical and not strategic.

Chances are you've seen a leader gather the team to praise someone. And I bet the praise was focused more on fire *fighting* than fire *prevention*.

The recognitions I've seen (and admittedly, have called out myself) are usually a heroic, last-minute effort to solve a problem, fix a mistake, or recover from a customer-service error. Some examples:

- The materials for a program were never shipped or were sent to the wrong state. A team member jumps into their car and drives through the night to deliver them just in time. (Here's a $100 Visa card for you!)

- You landed a large client opportunity but need to staff up to serve it. As a result, a team member is asked to take on several roles until you can post the needed positions, interview dozens of people, make the hires, and get them trained. (Here's dinner out on us—in a month, when you can actually go, and assuming you've not quit by then.)

- You've announced the global availability of a new product. The only problem is, it isn't completely finished and requires a final pilot, quality testing, package refinements, handwork, and assembly. Now you're putting people on planes to deliver hot-off-the-press materials because you burned through your three-week buffer. (Here's a pair of movie tickets for you and your significant other, assuming they're still with you.)

I used to be a regular competitor in a car/foot race called the "Delta Dash"—dropping off packages at the Delta airport outpost so they could be delivered across the country in 5 hours. (You likely have to be of a certain generation to remember this.) Today entire industries exist to accommodate our pull toward urgency. (Ever use an expedited passport service?) One of the key competencies to protect your team against urgencies is discernment (a.k.a. good judgment). Making sound decisions that align your team's time and energy with their Wildly Important Goals (see Challenge 23) will reduce the temptation of rushing to the "urgent" (unless your team works in an emergency room and/or I've pulled a hamstring doing the Delta Dash and need immediate attention). I'll go into more detail about what's meant by "Wildly Important Goals" in that challenge, but for now, it's vital to reduce the tension between the important and the urgent. Finding harmony between the two is often a delicate balancing act. It can help to take a hard look at the pants-on-fire division leader down the hall and decide that's not your path or brand.

As leaders, we can help protect our teams against urgencies by identifying and rewarding the specific behaviors that lead to achieving our goals. But first, we need to ensure we haven't modeled or reinforced a culture that rewards firefighting more than fire prevention. That's not to say urgencies don't sometimes happen.

The other extreme is to try to eliminate the reality of urgencies altogether. I once worked with an associate who, with a straight face, announced, "I don't work in urgent mode. Ever. I *only* work on projects that are thought out, planned, and scheduled." I remember thinking, *Well, great for you—and you'll never work for me*. Truth be told, I'm certain she had no intention of working for me. Perhaps we were both on the extremes at the time.

Protect your team against urgencies by recognizing the behaviors you want to model and reward. It's your responsibility to focus your team members on the "wildly important" (important and proactive efforts) and not the wildfires—even the ones you set!

FROM MESS TO SUCCESS:
PROTECT YOUR TEAM AGAINST URGENCIES

- Recognize that you may well be the source of many team urgencies. How do they show up?

- How will you plan better or say no to more?

1. Ask yourself if your need for validation or excitement is undermining the focus of your team.
2. Assign reasonable due dates to future initiatives.
3. Reward proactive and preventative efforts, not just heroic firefighting.

Day 1	Day 2	Day 3	Day 4	Day 5
Demonstrate Humility	Think Abundantly	Listen First	Declare Your Intent	Make and Keep Commitments
Day 6	Day 7	Day 8	Day 9	Day 10
Carry Your Own Weather	Inspire Trust	Model Work/Life Balance	Place the Right People in the Right Roles	Make Time for Relationships
Day 11	Day 12	Day 13	Day 14	Day 15
Check Your Paradigms	Lead Difficult Conversations	Talk Straight	Balance Courage and Consideration	Show Loyalty
Day 16	Day 17	Day 18	Day 19	Day 20
Make It Safe to Tell the Truth	Right Wrongs	Coach Continuously	Protect Your Team Against Urgencies	Hold Regular 1-on-1s
Day 21	Day 22	Day 23	Day 24	Day 25
Allow Others to Be Smart	Create Vision	Identify the Wildly Important Goals® (WIGs®)	Align Actions with the Wildly Important Goals	Ensure Your Systems Support Your Mission
Day 26	Day 27	Day 28	Day 29	Day 30
Deliver Results	Celebrate Wins	Make High-Value Decisions	Lead Through Change	Get Better

CHALLENGE 20

HOLD REGULAR
1-ON-1s

What's preventing you from holding
1-on-1s with each of your team members?

In keeping with the previous challenge's fire theme, most leaders operate from either a fire prevention or a firefighting inclination. I've written much of this book from the perspective of fire prevention—that's where efficiency meets effectiveness in the long term—but as you know, my natural tendency is to want to fight fires.

> ...IF I ASKED YOU TO LIST YOUR MOST IMPORTANT ASSETS, MOST (IF NOT ALL) OF YOU WOULD START WITH YOUR PEOPLE. IN THE LONG RUN, NOTHING IS MORE IMPORTANT THAN THE PEOPLE YOU LEAD (AND KNOWING HOW TO LEAD THEM), AND YOU KNOW IT. BUT HOW YOU SHOW THAT IMPORTANCE CAN BE RADICALLY DIFFERENT FROM HOW THEY PERCEIVE IT.

Let's face it, many of us love the challenge of an urgency, get an adrenaline rush running toward the flames, and seek the accolades from saving the day. And if you're one of those leaders, you're probably terrible at holding regular 1-on-1s. Consider me the poster boy for what a management mess looks like for this challenge. (Note: Nowhere did I promise *all* my messes had become successes.)

We firefighting leaders are addicted to urgency. And because of our addiction, we're good at disappointing people. I'm constantly canceling my 1-on-1s: the can't-miss morning meeting went long, I got held up in the hallway by a colleague needing my advice, and now my phone is ringing. It's the call I've been waiting for, from an important author asking for a book blurb, a famous executive who wants to appear on my *Great Life, Great Career* radio program, or a thought leader we want to interview. Important stuff. Really important. Honestly, more important than my 1-on-1 (but is it really?). Truth be told, it's a little painful seeing my direct report through my office window, holding a folder full of things they're excited to share. I bet they've been preparing for the meeting all week—gathering work samples and saying no to conflicting meetings, eager to make a good impression. This meeting is important to them.

And it's important to me too. Just not *as* important as everything else ging on. That's the brutal truth. The word "hypocrite" comes to mind, but I push it down and text my assistant to cancel the meeting. My assistant has a lot of muscle memory around this task, and the associate nods and walks off. Meanwhile, I've answered the call and I'm back to doing important leadership stuff. Candidly, I've been on both sides of this situation and should know better because it sucks.

But if I asked you to list your most important assets, most (if not all) of you would start with your people. In the long run, nothing is more important than the people you lead (and knowing how to lead them), and you know it. But how you show that importance can be radically different from how they perceive it.

There's a parallel to this with families. I recently interviewed Julie Morgenstern, bestselling author of many books, including *Time to Parent*, and she shared the differing perceptions between children and their parents. For example, a common dialogue goes something like this:

Parent: "I sacrificed everything for you. I worked and saved money for years, provided you with every necessity: food, shelter, clothing, transportation. You wanted for nothing."

Kid: "Yeah, but you were never there for me!"

The parent, well aware of all the "invisible" actions they do to support their child, feels they have done "everything" to provide for them. But the child never saw those invisible actions; they just wanted time together.

Sound familiar? As a leader, you know how many "invisible" hours you've dedicated to the success of your team. But what they need from you is time. They need 1-on-1s, to be specific, so they can bring up issues hindering their progress, get feedback and coaching, create a development plan, and problem-solve with you. 1-on-1 meetings are one of your most important tools for increasing your team's engagement. So we need to hold them, even in the face of legitimate challenges and constant urgencies.

Several challenges in this book lay the foundation for holding regular 1-on-1s, including:

- Demonstrate Humility

- Declare Your Intent

- Make and Keep Commitments

- Inspire Trust

- Take Time for Relationships

- Check Your Paradigms

Several challenges also relate directly to *how* to conduct a 1-on-1:

- Listen First

- Lead Difficult Conversations

- Talk Straight

- Balance Courage and Consideration

- Make It Safe to Tell the Truth

- Coach Continuously

- Allow Others to Be Smart

- Create Vision

- Identify the Wildly Important Goals (WIGs)

Nearly half of the leadership challenges in this book either directly support or are magnified through the 1-on-1 meeting. Holding 1-on-1s is not a burden or a part of some leadership checklist. It's a value. Until we see it as such, we'll continue to falter in our attempts to hold them. And if our calendar doesn't match our values, one of them is off.

My advice (to both of us) is to be realistic about how often we can hold regular 1-on-1s. Don't announce you'll hold weekly 1-on-1s and then cancel them. This is an issue of quality over quantity, especially when the firehouse siren goes off. Start slow by gathering your team together and declaring your intent. You might say something such as:

"I'd like to start holding regular 1-on-1s, starting with once a month so that you can get coaching, share successes, and bring up issues that affect your engagement. I may occasionally have to cancel because something requires my immediate attention. Please pre-forgive me if this happens, and release yourself from the belief that you aren't a priority. I'll do my best to honor the commitment and make this time valuable for both of us; please do your best to be prepared and flexible."

FranklinCovey has a point of view on how to structure 1-on-1s, starting with the fact that it's your associate's meeting, not yours. Also, you should do 30 percent of the talking compared to their 70 percent, because after all, it's their agenda, not yours. Don't confuse this with your regularly scheduled team or staff meeting where the agenda can typically be all yours. In our book *Everyone Deserves a Great Manager: The 6 Critical Practices for Leading a Team*, we dedicate an entire practice to holding effective 1-on-1s. The lead author, I hear, is a total management mess (so be warned).

I may have written this challenge for myself. The more like me you are, the more I hope this resonates. And if you're on my team and reading this chapter, I fully expect you'll keep me accountable too.

FROM MESS TO SUCCESS:
HOLD REGULAR 1-ON-1s

- If you struggle with holding 1-on-1s, commit to starting slow. Recognize that, for most leaders, once a month is only suggested because it's better than not holding 1-on-1s at all. A weekly cadence is more ideal. There are many variables that will impact your frequency. Acknowledging them up front is crucial to your credibility and managing expectations.

- Declare your intent with your team.

- Before the 1-on-1:

  1. Review one of this book's related challenges and bring that skill into the meeting.
  2. Keep in mind that your team member will "own" the agenda.

- During the 1-on-1:

  1. Commit to do no more than 30 percent of the talking. Find out what you can do to support your team member. Remember, coach, don't tell.
  2. Seek and give feedback as appropriate.
  3. A minimum of thirty minutes is recommended to realistically accommodate key status updates and "clear the path" items.
  4. Devote time to development planning and career-path discussions.

Day 1	Day 2	Day 3	Day 4	Day 5
Demonstrate Humility	Think Abundantly	Listen First	Declare Your Intent	Make and Keep Commitments
Day 6	**Day 7**	**Day 8**	**Day 9**	**Day 10**
Carry Your Own Weather	Inspire Trust	Model Work/Life Balance	Place the Right People in the Right Roles	Make Time for Relationships
Day 11	**Day 12**	**Day 13**	**Day 14**	**Day 15**
Check Your Paradigms	Lead Difficult Conversations	Talk Straight	Balance Courage and Consideration	Show Loyalty
Day 16	**Day 17**	**Day 18**	**Day 19**	**Day 20**
Make It Safe to Tell the Truth	Right Wrongs	Coach Continuously	Protect Your Team Against Urgencies	Hold Regular 1-on-1s
Day 21	**Day 22**	**Day 23**	**Day 24**	**Day 25**
Allow Others to Be Smart	Create Vision	Identify the Wildly Important Goals® (WIGs®)	Align Actions with the Wildly Important Goals	Ensure Your Systems Support Your Mission
Day 26	**Day 27**	**Day 28**	**Day 29**	**Day 30**
Deliver Results	Celebrate Wins	Make High-Value Decisions	Lead Through Change	Get Better

CHALLENGE 21

ALLOW OTHERS TO BE SMART

Do you need to be the smartest
person in the room?

What's it like being in a professional relationship with you? Consider how your colleagues and team members would answer these questions:

- Do you feel better and more encouraged after being with me?
- Are you lifted or diminished from talking to me?
- Can you tell stories without me "one-upping" you?
- Can you share new ideas with me?
- Can you win, or even survive, a debate with me, or do I fatigue you to the point of surrender? .
- Do I always have to be right, have the final word, and the winning idea?
- Can you feel smart in my presence?
- Do I leave time for others to speak, challenge, or brainstorm?

Ask a peer, a direct report, your leader, your spouse or partner, or a fellow committee member what it's like to know you. Consider their answers in light of this leadership challenge—do you encourage and allow others to be smart? During the early days of leading the marketing department, I was comfortable with the way we conducted business—direct mail, email, phone calls, face-to-face meetings, a decent website, live preview events, etc. But as time passed, our buyers and influencers were increasingly savvy about sourcing our industry's solutions through digital channels. It was way past time for me to onboard significant talent to grow our digital capabilities.

We needed to recruit associates from outside the firm to augment our expertise in new strategies like SEO, UX, marketing automation, video production, social media, and the ever-changing landscape that is B2B marketing. I needed to hire specialists who on Day One knew more about their roles than I ever would. We hired some very talented industry professionals with deep expertise in narrow but vital areas and I felt myself becoming less relevant by the day. Or at least that was my perception.

In Liz Wiseman's profound leadership book *Multipliers: How the Best Leaders Make Everyone Smarter*, she invites leaders to assess several key questions: Are you the genius, or the genius maker? Are you a Multiplier (someone who uses their intelligence to bring out the best in others), or a Diminisher (the "smartest person in the room" who shuts everyone else down)?

Dr. Covey endorsed few books in his lifetime and wrote the foreword to even fewer. I'm proud of him for penning Liz's foreword. This book is a masterpiece on understanding our natural tendency as leaders to always have the answers. I can honestly attribute changing my leadership style to her book. I chose to step back and empower this team of geniuses to run with their strengths. As a result, they grew our digital presence to best-of-class (all while I confused Instagram and Pinterest and tried in vain to understand why a buyer would look for us on either). It wasn't easy to move from being respected as one of the most creative and forward-thinking leaders to just trying to keep up with these new minds, all much younger and, truthfully, much smarter in their areas of expertise.

Plainly stated, before my Multiplier "aha" moment, I didn't always do a stellar job of empowering my team to lead out, craft strategy, and allocate resources. I maintained my authority and stature by serving as the gatekeeper for who spoke to the CEO and executive team and who didn't. In hindsight, I probably stifled some creativity and skill development in others and didn't ignite the level of progress that could have happened, had I been more secure in my own contributions. I learned that my job was not to know everything, but to identify, attract and, most important, engage those who did, and take us to the next level. Some will think I succeeded; others will think I failed. Welcome to leadership.

Leaders who struggle with allowing others to be smart are often driven by their ego, insecurities, or a desire to jump in and top any idea. The Marketing Division at FranklinCovey used to have a saying: "The best idea wins—as long as it's Scott's." (It was a joke, I hope, and I'd like to keep it that way.) Here are three skills you can use to empower and engage others to showcase their creativity, experience, and perspectives:

IN LIZ WISEMAN'S PROFOUND LEADERSHIP BOOK, *MULTIPLIERS: HOW THE BEST LEADERS MAKE EVERYONE SMARTER*, SHE INVITES LEADERS TO ASSESS SEVERAL KEY QUESTIONS: ARE YOU THE GENIUS, OR THE GENIUS MAKER? ARE YOU A MULTIPLIER (SOMEONE WHO USES THEIR INTELLIGENCE TO BRING OUT THE BEST IN OTHERS), OR A DIMINISHER (THE "SMARTEST PERSON IN THE ROOM" WHO SHUTS EVERYONE ELSE DOWN)?

- Consider the percentage of time you spend talking versus listening. This means more than just "hearing" the other person—more than the physics and mechanism of absorbing, interpreting, and making meaning from sound. I'm talking about really listening—applying focused attention to the other person and what they're saying. Listening is not just hearing, but understanding and caring about what is said.

- Decide when to be the expert with the "right" answer, and when to allow your team to work through the process of coming up with it themselves. Many leaders assume their job is to provide the right answer as quickly as possible. Often that's the case. But sometimes it's more important that your team struggle with the process of getting there themselves so their capacity to do it again is increased.

- Step back from being the driver of the discussion. Ask someone on your team to take the lead.

FROM MESS TO SUCCESS:
ALLOW OTHERS TO BE SMART

- Read *Multipliers* and take the complimentary online assessment that comes with the book purchase. It will rock your world and help you become a genius maker. Your future employees will thank you for it.

- Assess your paradigm: Are you comfortable surrounding yourself with people who are smarter? Do you hire down to keep your stature high, or do you hire up to raise the quality and success output of all your initiatives?

- During your next 1-on-1 with a team member, ask them to sincerely tell you what it's like being in a professional relationship with you.

- Invite a team member to lead a project meeting (with or without you in attendance). Step back and stay out of their way.

- The next time you lead a meeting, ask a trusted colleague to take inventory of the percentage of time you talked and solved problems, etc. Given your awareness that the inventory is taking place, the time you spend leading might be less than normal. But it could still be instructive and give insight into any accidental diminishing tendencies you might have.

PART 3

GET RESULTS

Day 1 Demonstrate Humility	**Day 2** Think Abundantly	**Day 3** Listen First	**Day 4** Declare Your Intent	**Day 5** Make and Keep Commitments
Day 6 Carry Your Own Weather	**Day 7** Inspire Trust	**Day 8** Model Work/Life Balance	**Day 9** Place the Right People in the Right Roles	**Day 10** Make Time for Relationships
Day 11 Check Your Paradigms	**Day 12** Lead Difficult Conversations	**Day 13** Talk Straight	**Day 14** Balance Courage and Consideration	**Day 15** Show Loyalty
Day 16 Make It Safe to Tell the Truth	**Day 17** Right Wrongs	**Day 18** Coach Continuously	**Day 19** Protect Your Team Against Urgencies	**Day 20** Hold Regular 1-on-1s
Day 21 Allow Others to Be Smart	**Day 22** Create Vision	**Day 23** Identify the Wildly Important Goals® (WIGs®)	**Day 24** Align Actions with the Wildly Important Goals	**Day 25** Ensure Your Systems Support Your Mission
Day 26 Deliver Results	**Day 27** Celebrate Wins	**Day 28** Make High-Value Decisions	**Day 29** Lead Through Change	**Day 30** Get Better

CHALLENGE 22

CREATE VISION

Have you articulated an inspiring vision so
your people choose to volunteer their best?

In modern history, Walt Disney has been one of the most brilliant business leaders at creating and communicating a vision.

Celebration, the Disney Development Company's master-planned community, is a superb example. It was the fulfillment of Walt's dream, partially achieved through EPCOT Center, at Walt Disney World in Orlando, Florida. I happen to know its story well, as I was one of the founding team members on the project from 1992 to 1996. In a few short years, Disney transformed 10 square miles of open land and cow pasture into one of the most innovative towns in the world. Celebration showcased a first-of-its-kind public/private school, a collection of retail stores, homes and apartments, a progressive hospital, and office buildings designed by many of the world's premier architects. The town offers state-of-the-art technology supporting a lifestyle described by some as "where *The Jetsons* meets Mayberry."

Celebration isn't perfect, of course, but that's not the point. All of it was inspired by one person's vision—someone I assume most of the team members had never met. That was the power of Walt Disney's vision; a dream he communicated with passion, clarity, and consistency.

MY EXPERIENCE WORKING AT DISNEY TAUGHT ME THAT CREATING A VISION IS BOLD AND OFTEN UNCOMFORTABLE. IT CAN BE BOTH INSPIRING AND A REAL STRETCH... LEADERS CREATE VISION UNTIL IT'S SHARED BY THEIR TEAMS AND COLLEAGUES. THEY DEPICT A VISION SO CLEAR AND ALIGNED TO THE ORGANIZATIONAL MISSION AND GOALS THAT ANYONE COULD COMMUNICATE IT IN THIRTY SECONDS OR LESS.

My experience working at Disney taught me that creating a bold vision is often uncomfortable. It can be both inspiring and a real stretch. Personally, I've always excelled at creating vision, and count it as one of my most valuable leadership strengths. And I'm not just talking about *having* a vision—that's not the name of this challenge. Leaders *create* vision until it's shared by their teams and colleagues. They depict a vision so clear and aligned to the organizational mission and goals that anyone could communicate it in thirty seconds or less.

Conventional learning theory suggests that individuals are either visual, auditory, or kinesthetic learners. I actually believe that, unless you have a sight impairment, *everyone* is a visual learner. Nobody ever secured a construction loan without a blueprint, and the same applies to leaders. Whether you use PowerPoint, pictures, models, or storyboards, creating vision requires others to *see* it. And because you can't climb into someone's head and know if they see (and understand) your vision, you must ensure that people can articulate it. I'll ask my colleagues and team members to do just that—repeat back to me the vision I just shared. Often they'll bring something new to it as they do. And that's great, because creating a vision is often a group endeavor.

In my previous role as chief marketing officer, I was responsible for creating a compelling vision around numerous events and initiatives, including Facilitator Enhancement Day (or FED). This event allowed our client facilitators (more than five thousand certified every year) to increase their business acumen, network, and improve their facilitation skills. Every year, our team created a compelling marketing campaign with a theme, website, email strategies, and print invitations to support the FED. We completed this long list of tasks nearly a year before the event so client partners could communicate the experience to their customers. The fact that the collateral had been designed and distributed before the agenda was locked would frustrate other areas of the business: "How can you sell something before you create it?" they would ask. The answer was simple: When you can create and articulate a powerful vision, you've improved the likelihood that it will come to fruition. This happens all the time, such as in the movie industry, where marketing teams create a trailer while the production process is still going on. It's common for a film to be in final editing literally days before it arrives at your local theater.

The mistake is assuming that your work is done after you create that powerful vision. You may be familiar with the recent debacle of the Fyre Festival. The organizers created a masterful vision of an exclusive, high-end music festival on a secluded Caribbean island, with beautiful people, live bands, and luxury boats in turquoise water. The festival organizers paid hundreds of thousands of dollars to "influencers" to share the vision through social media.

The only problem was that the vision was completely disconnected from reality.

When attendees to the sold-out event arrived, they discovered repurposed hurricane tents instead of luxury villas, and cheese sandwiches instead of gourmet catering. The event collapsed into a chaotic rush as attendees tried to flee the island. Truly, a great vision isn't enough.

Effective leaders structure a vision, implement it, and bring it to life, which our organization teaches in *The 4 Essential Roles of Leadership* work session. At a high level, creating a vision means defining where your team is going and how they will get there. Notice the "how" part. It's not unusual for a leader, after a grand pronouncement, to sit back and assume their vision will happen. In truth, many bold strategies never reach liftoff because team members were either confused, uninspired, or had a "this too shall pass" attitude.

Creating a vision, effectively communicating it, and translating it into daily behaviors requires many talents. The good news is that they're learnable:

- Adapt your message to the culture. Are you speaking the same language as your audience? Are you using terms everyone understands? Can others see themselves in the message?

- Craft a vision that is within reach. A bold aspiration to colonize Mars in two years sounds dumb. Calibrate your vision so that people need to stretch—perhaps significantly—but can still win. The vision must be accomplishable.

- Articulate and repeat the vision at every appropriate opportunity. Do this until you've communicated the vision so many times, you can't stand to hear it yourself. Even when you're fatigued by your own vision, you're likely 50 percent of the way there. Don't make the fatal mistake of believing just because it's clear in your mind, it's clear in the minds of others. Vision becomes a reality with relentless pursuit and relentless communication.

- Create ambassadors. Gather colleagues to communicate your vision, ensuring they understand. Don't patronize them, but have them repeat it back to you. Have them ask questions, push on you, think of all the what-ifs. The more your ambassadors understand, the more likely they'll become faithful translators and champions. Consider recording yourself via video and audio, and also articulating your vision in writing so everyone understands it point by point.

Some of this advice may seem pedantic, but the goal is to reinforce the reality that no leader has ever overcommunicated an inspiring vision. Worthy aspirational projects and initiatives typically fail because leadership wrongly thought they had been sufficiently translated throughout the team or organization. Or in some cases, they lost interest themselves.

AT A HIGH LEVEL, CREATING A VISION MEANS DEFINING WHERE YOUR TEAM IS GOING AND HOW THEY WILL GET THERE. NOTICE THE "HOW" PART. IT'S NOT UNUSUAL FOR A LEADER, AFTER A GRAND PRONOUNCEMENT, TO SIT BACK AND ASSUME THEIR VISION WILL HAPPEN.

FROM MESS TO SUCCESS:
CREATE VISION

- Draft a team vision by answering these questions:

  1. What contributions can our team make to the organization's mission and vision?
  2. If our team could make one extraordinary contribution over the next one to five years, what would it be?

- Take a moment to remember an inspiring vision that resonated with you. What about it made it personally motivating and powerful?

- Create a vision for your team by articulating not only the why and the what, but the how. The how may well be the key that brings it to success.

Day 1	Day 2	Day 3	Day 4	Day 5
Demonstrate Humility	Think Abundantly	Listen First	Declare Your Intent	Make and Keep Commitments
Day 6	**Day 7**	**Day 8**	**Day 9**	**Day 10**
Carry Your Own Weather	Inspire Trust	Model Work/Life Balance	Place the Right People in the Right Roles	Make Time for Relationships
Day 11	**Day 12**	**Day 13**	**Day 14**	**Day 15**
Check Your Paradigms	Lead Difficult Conversations	Talk Straight	Balance Courage and Consideration	Show Loyalty
Day 16	**Day 17**	**Day 18**	**Day 19**	**Day 20**
Make It Safe to Tell the Truth	Right Wrongs	Coach Continuously	Protect Your Team Against Urgencies	Hold Regular 1-on-1s
Day 21	**Day 22**	**Day 23**	**Day 24**	**Day 25**
Allow Others to Be Smart	Create Vision	Identify the Wildly Important Goals® (WIGs®)	Align Actions with the Wildly Important Goals	Ensure Your Systems Support Your Mission
Day 26	**Day 27**	**Day 28**	**Day 29**	**Day 30**
Deliver Results	Celebrate Wins	Make High-Value Decisions	Lead Through Change	Get Better

CHALLENGE 23

IDENTIFY THE WILDLY IMPORTANT GOALS (WIGs)

Does everyone know the team's top two
or three priorities (WIGs) and how they will
align their efforts to achieve them?

More is not better; better is better. Unless it's pizza; then, let's face it, pizza is always better in quantity. The temptation to say yes to more of the great (even good) ideas that come our way might be the biggest trap leaders fall into. Have I fallen into the "say yes" pit? Without a doubt. I've also set up residence and had my mail forwarded there. I love to say yes. But what I've had to learn the hard way is to prioritize saying yes to Wildly Important Goals and not to a host of other good ideas. Wildly Important Goals (or WIGs, as we refer to them) are the few, highly important goals that must be achieved, or no other goal matters. Despite their critical importance, WIGs can be neglected because of the temptation to focus on the urgencies of the day (see Challenge 19).

> MORE IS NOT BETTER. BETTER IS BETTER. UNLESS IT'S PIZZA. THEN, LET'S FACE IT, PIZZA IS ALWAYS BETTER IN QUANTITY. THE TEMPTATION TO SAY YES TO MORE OF THE GREAT (EVEN GOOD) IDEAS THAT COME OUR WAY MIGHT BE THE BIGGEST TRAP LEADERS FALL INTO.

One way to get swallowed up by urgencies is to focus on too many new ideas. Not long ago, while reading *Multipliers*, I had a professional epiphany. I came to understand that I'm what the author terms "The Idea Guy"— one of six types of Accidental Diminishers (a concept previously referenced in Challenge 21). The Idea Guy always wants more, says more, creates more, and offers more to others. It's how they've proven their value in the past: by always having multiple solutions, typically sold with charisma and flair, that smart and focused people often love to follow.

At first, the Idea Guy wins, getting the budget, time, attention, focus, and resources to save the day with their plan. They're seen as relevant in the moment (because they are) and their heroic efforts takes the organization closer to some objective, at least on the surface. But here's the issue: Too often such ideas, although often exceptionally creative and compelling in solving immediate short-term problems, can distract from the organizational WIGs. This isn't to say creative people (a.k.a. the Idea Guy) aren't integral to any organization's need to innovate. They're likely invaluable; they just may need guidance and discipline.

I suspect the author was thinking of me when she created this type (or perhaps it was you?). The leadership competency to work with us Idea Guys is discernment—to balance our energy and drive with the longer-term must-do initiatives. Often that balance means being able to say no to the next new and tempting idea. I'll wager few of us really ever think of the downstream impact our casual yes creates. Great leaders learn not to dismiss, but rather leverage, the Idea Guy's talents against the WIGs.

So just how do you identify the WIGs for your team? Don't start by asking, "What are the most important things to focus on?" As more fully outlined in *The 4 Disciplines of Execution*, the bestselling book by Chris McChesney, Sean Covey, and Jim Huling, ask, "If every other area of

> WILDLY IMPORTANT GOALS (OR WIGs, AS WE REFER TO THEM) ARE THE FEW, HIGHLY IMPORTANT GOALS THAT MUST BE ACHIEVED, OR NO OTHER GOAL MATTERS.

our operation remained at its current level of performance, what is the one area where change would have the greatest impact?" This will help you generate a list of potential WIGs. Then share them with your team for input and consensus.

To increase the likelihood of achieving your WIGs:

- *Collaborate*. Work with key stakeholders to identify and then debate whether your WIGs are worthy of the stature. Ask, "When executed, do these WIGs provide return that justifies displacing other goals?" Remember, every goal can't be wildly important.

- *Choose*. Select the initiatives you *won't* be working on. Share with your team what you're saying no to so they value what you're saying yes to.

- *Craft*. Construct your goals in clear, actionable language. *The 4 Disciplines of Execution* teaches a simple formula we call "From X to Y by When." For example, *We will move client retention from 84 to 91 percent by December 31*.

- *Communicate*. Share your goals with enough clarity that all involved can evangelize for them with the same gravitas and understanding you do.

- *Track*. Keep a record of the progress you make toward your goals. Use a visually compelling scoreboard so anyone can tell at a glance if you're winning or losing against the goal.

- *Delegate*. Ensure that every team member involved with executing the goal understands their contribution, and what new and perhaps different behaviors they need to engage in. Be mindful of what you need to do differently as well.

- *Meet*. Plan and lead recurring meetings to check on the status of the goal and scoreboard, report wins and misses, and make further commitments to accomplish the WIG.

- *Celebrate*. Identify successes when the WIG is achieved. Then add the next one to the list.

I used to be notorious in our executive team meetings for asking, when an opportunity or a challenging situation arose, "Well, what if we…?" So much so, it could be the epitaph on my headstone. This was historically my preamble to a deluge of creative (but distracting) ideas. When I made a conscious effort to focus on WIGs, I committed that I would stop using that simple phrase so often, which has allowed much of our organization to stay focused on our WIGs. This can be a hard habit to break, especially if you're an Idea Guy like me.

FROM MESS TO SUCCESS:
IDENTIFY THE WILDLY IMPORTANT GOALS

- With your team, determine which two to three priorities *must* be achieved, otherwise nothing else you do will matter.

- Determine a starting line, finish line, and deadline for each WIG: "From X to Y by When."

- Align the WIGs with your organization's vision, mission, and strategy.

- Follow the sage advice of business author Jim Collins and put as much focus on your "not-to-do" list as you put on your "to-do" list.

Day 1	Day 2	Day 3	Day 4	Day 5
Demonstrate Humility	Think Abundantly	Listen First	Declare Your Intent	Make and Keep Commitments
Day 6	Day 7	Day 8	Day 9	Day 10
Carry Your Own Weather	Inspire Trust	Model Work/Life Balance	Place the Right People in the Right Roles	Make Time for Relationships
Day 11	Day 12	Day 13	Day 14	Day 15
Check Your Paradigms	Lead Difficult Conversations	Talk Straight	Balance Courage and Consideration	Show Loyalty
Day 16	Day 17	Day 18	Day 19	Day 20
Make It Safe to Tell the Truth	Right Wrongs	Coach Continuously	Protect Your Team Against Urgencies	Hold Regular 1-on-1s
Day 21	Day 22	Day 23	Day 24	Day 25
Allow Others to Be Smart	Create Vision	Identify the Wildly Important Goals® (WIGs®)	Align Actions with the Wildly Important Goals	Ensure Your Systems Support Your Mission
Day 26	Day 27	Day 28	Day 29	Day 30
Deliver Results	Celebrate Wins	Make High-Value Decisions	Lead Through Change	Get Better

CHALLENGE 24

ALIGN ACTIONS WITH THE WILDLY IMPORTANT GOALS

Are the efforts of your team members moving your goals forward? How can you make it easier for them to do so?

The previous challenge dealt with identifying and sharing Wildly Important Goals (WIGs) with your team. This challenge focuses on actually getting the WIGs accomplished. The goal is to focus everyone's actions so they're in alignment with and in service to the WIG. But that raises a simple question: Do you and your team members know what those actions (behaviors) should be?

If a goal is elevated to WIG status, it's vital to the team's and the organization's survival or growth. That also means every goal your team is trying to realize can't be a WIG, as that dilutes the significance and commitment to marshal a heightened level of focus, time, resources, and attention. Here's another formula to keep in mind: Every Goal Is a WIG = You're a Fraud.

You've likely heard (and probably shared) the saying, "Insanity is repeating the same thing over and over again and expecting different results." Ignoring the fact that Albert Einstein probably never said this, it's still pretty darn relevant. For leaders, aligning to WIGs means everyone involved needs to change behaviors. To quote Dr. Covey, "Says easy, does hard."

> MEANINGFUL CHANGE COMES FROM THE INSIDE OUT. IT HAS TO START WITH YOU AS THE LEADER, COMMITTING TO AND THEN ENACTING NEW BEHAVIORS. WHEN YOU CHANGE YOUR BEHAVIOR, OTHERS WILL SEE YOUR COMMITMENT TO ACCOMPLISHING THE WIG.

Meaningful change comes from the inside out. It has to start with you as the leader, committing to and then enacting new behaviors. When you change your behavior, others will see your commitment to accomplishing the WIG. You can choose to raise the stakes by announcing how you intend to change your behavior at the start of a new goal. Such a strategy comes with both high risk and high reward. People will watch. And then watch some more. They'll continue until you exhibit the behavior so consistently, it's accepted as the new normal; or you get bored or otherwise give up and you're exposed as a hypocrite. Choose a change in behavior that's at the same level you want to see in your team members, unless your role is more removed or narrowly defined. A chief marketing officer is likely to engage with a WIG at a very different level than a digital-content manager or social-media director. The commonality is new and better behavior on display for all to see.

To further ensure your team has aligned the right actions to the WIGs, meet and brainstorm the specific behaviors you need from each other. This may feel patronizing at first, but leaving others to blindly guess what they should do is abdicating your responsibility as a leader. Even the most seasoned and mature individuals may need help understanding what "new" looks like for them. As is often heard around the halls of our organization, "No involvement, no commitment."

Here are a few specific things you can do to keep your actions aligned with your WIGs (drawn from FranklinCovey's bestselling book, *The 4 Disciplines of Execution*):

- Focus your finest efforts on the one or two goals that will make the greatest impact (rather than giving mediocre effort to dozens of goals).

- Choose the battles that win the war. It's easy to generate a long list of to-do items in support of your WIGs. Rather, ask, "What are the fewest number of battles necessary to win this war?" Focus your attention on the critical items that will get you the victory.

- Veto but don't dictate. Allow your leaders and team members to define the actions that will support your WIGs. Your role is to bring clarity; the leaders below you will bring engagement (if you allow them to).

- Have a finish line in the form of *From X to Y by When*. In order to ensure your actions are aligned to your WIG, you must have a clearly measurable result and date by which the result must be achieved. Although we addressed this concept in a previous challenge, it bears repeating, based on its proven success and impact with clients.

When I've watched leaders successfully align their actions to their WIGs, they've done more than trumpeted a new motivational kickoff—they made fundamental shifts in how they planned their weeks and days and how they staffed and used resources. The resulting growth in personal maturity, business acumen, and influence has been remarkable. They also earn the satisfaction of hitting the "must have" goals. And isn't that what every leader has been charged with doing?

FROM MESS TO SUCCESS:
ALIGN ACTIONS WITH THE WILDLY IMPORTANT GOALS

- With your team, brainstorm specific behaviors that will help them accomplish your Wildly Important Goals.

- To achieve new and different results, everyone will likely need to learn something new and do something different. Show the courage to ask your team members to identify any new behaviors they think *you* should implement to progress the WIG. This may help them be more receptive to suggestions you make regarding their behaviors.

- Lead out on your own new and better behavior and use it to coach, not shame, others.

- Ensure team players have the big-picture perspective, not only a myopic view of just their part.

Day 1	Day 2	Day 3	Day 4	Day 5
Demonstrate Humility	Think Abundantly	Listen First	Declare Your Intent	Make and Keep Commitments
Day 6	**Day 7**	**Day 8**	**Day 9**	**Day 10**
Carry Your Own Weather	Inspire Trust	Model Work/Life Balance	Place the Right People in the Right Roles	Make Time for Relationships
Day 11	**Day 12**	**Day 13**	**Day 14**	**Day 15**
Check Your Paradigms	Lead Difficult Conversations	Talk Straight	Balance Courage and Consideration	Show Loyalty
Day 16	**Day 17**	**Day 18**	**Day 19**	**Day 20**
Make It Safe to Tell the Truth	Right Wrongs	Coach Continuously	Protect Your Team Against Urgencies	Hold Regular 1-on-1s
Day 21	**Day 22**	**Day 23**	**Day 24**	**Day 25**
Allow Others to Be Smart	Create Vision	Identify the Wildly Important Goals® (WIGs®)	Align Actions with the Wildly Important Goals	Ensure Your Systems Support Your Mission
Day 26	**Day 27**	**Day 28**	**Day 29**	**Day 30**
Deliver Results	Celebrate Wins	Make High-Value Decisions	Lead Through Change	Get Better

CHALLENGE 25

ENSURE YOUR SYSTEMS SUPPORT YOUR MISSION

Effective leaders create systems that make
it easier to achieve results. When was the
last time you did a "systems check"?

Have you ever made an independent, conscious decision to stop using your current toothpaste and use a different brand? I'm talking about a decision that was all you—no marketing, advertising, recommendations from friends, coupons, or free samples from the dentist. Probably not. And that likely has to do with human nature; we settle into patterns on the easy stuff so our brains can tackle bigger issues. I'm no neuroscientist, but I'm a proud owner of a brain, and this makes sense to me.

SOMETHING SIMILAR HAPPENS IN ORGANIZATIONS. WE SETTLE INTO ACCEPTABLE PATTERNS, ESPECIALLY AROUND AREAS OF THE BUSINESS THAT SEEM FINE.

Something similar happens in organizations. We settle into acceptable patterns, especially around areas of the business that seem fine. "Good enough" becomes "better left alone." We often step back and allow systems to just do their thing, even when they're not perfectly aligned to our mission and goals. Or we complain, which means the Operations Division becomes the company's scapegoat. Any system's many moving parts are never as simple as the complainers (that's you and me) think they are. Case in point: When my wife and I confront some system or process we don't understand, she'll ask: "Why don't they just do it *this* way?" To her immense frustration, I usually reply: "I'm sure they have their reasons. There's always more going on below the surface." Turns out we rarely, if ever, have all the facts—even after gathering the facts.

Systems are inherently complicated, even in small organizations. They're a necessary evil, kind of like broccoli (without cheese sauce). Annoying but necessary.

Organizational systems are everyone's responsibility. Not just to complain about, but to understand, support, and help improve. For example, if I think the price of a supplier is too high, I have the leadership responsibility to understand the current strategy. Assuming good intent on behalf of the system owner, I can then choose to schedule a meeting if I still have concerns. My advice is to choose these meetings carefully and be prepared to learn a bunch of facts you hadn't known before. When I've initiated these meetings, almost without fail I've ended up learning something that invalidated my brilliant solution for fixing everything. But I walked away with a better appreciation of *why* the system was in place and could articulate that to my team. My improved understanding helped my team accept the situation (and pick our battles more deliberately in the future.)

Not that I don't challenge and seek to improve our processes where I can. This is every leader's mandate: Change or die. Constantly improve your systems or be left behind. The hard truth is that some systems and processes seem to slow everything down. What sane person would design a system to slow something down? (Unless it's the brilliant mind who designed the Crock-Pot—thank you for my eight-hour, orange-glazed pork roast on winter Sundays. I love you.)

Think about this in terms of your own team—do your systems support your mission? Have you engaged the patience and due diligence to understand how your systems align or misalign to your strategies, your WIGs, and your client needs? How about your employees' needs? Consider the following systems-alignment questions:

- Are the right people with the right skills doing the right work?
- Are the right roles and responsibilities in place for people to work well together?
- Are people recognized and rewarded in the right way?
- Are the right resources available to succeed?
- Are the right decisions being made by the people closest to the work?
- Do we have the right processes in place to get the most important work done?

FranklinCovey's chief operations officer, Colleen Dom, has a saying to describe her team's role: "We don't define the company's strategy. Instead, we understand the strategy and create a system to enable it. We want to make sure we are not the business-prevention department."

I admire how Colleen and her team delicately manage four systemic tensions that keep our machine as lean and fast as possible:

- Support our clients in accomplishing their goals by adopting and implementing our solutions easily and affordably.
- Support our sales and delivery colleagues in ways that allow them to accomplish the above, earn a living, and stay engaged with our company.
- Protect the company and our intellectual property, brand, and reputation.
- Grow revenue and earn a profit for our shareholders.

While you likely don't have direct control over all the systems and processes you're working with, mindlessly accepting them as the status quo won't do. Your job is to understand the rationale for and nuances of any system that feels misaligned to your mission and goals, and influence (or, if you have the authority, make) improvements.

THIS IS EVERY LEADER'S MANDATE: CHANGE OR DIE. CONSTANTLY IMPROVE YOUR SYSTEMS OR BE LEFT BEHIND.

Although it's unlikely that your organizational mission will change, it's very likely that your systems will. Therefore, it may be necessary to perform periodic assessments to ensure both are in alignment. Efficiencies, new protocols, reduction of redundancies, etc., typically support improved profitability and simplicity. Just be certain these changes don't diminish your capacity or work against your ultimate goal of accomplishing your mission.

Who knows, you might even start liking broccoli after all (especially with the right support systems—namely, lemon juice, cheese sauce, salt, and a chocolate-milk chaser to wash it down).

FROM MESS TO SUCCESS:
ENSURE YOUR SYSTEMS SUPPORT YOUR MISSION

- Consider how existing systems support your company's mission, customers, sales force, brand, reputation, product development, and other vital functions.

- Identify one system that, if improved or streamlined, could have a disproportionately positive impact on multiple stakeholders.

- Take a deeper look at the aspects of that particular system that feel misaligned or overly burdensome. Perform your own due diligence to understand the nuances beneath the surface.

Day 1	Day 2	Day 3	Day 4	Day 5
Demonstrate Humility	Think Abundantly	Listen First	Declare Your Intent	Make and Keep Commitments
Day 6	**Day 7**	**Day 8**	**Day 9**	**Day 10**
Carry Your Own Weather	Inspire Trust	Model Work/Life Balance	Place the Right People in the Right Roles	Make Time for Relationships
Day 11	**Day 12**	**Day 13**	**Day 14**	**Day 15**
Check Your Paradigms	Lead Difficult Conversations	Talk Straight	Balance Courage and Consideration	Show Loyalty
Day 16	**Day 17**	**Day 18**	**Day 19**	**Day 20**
Make It Safe to Tell the Truth	Right Wrongs	Coach Continuously	Protect Your Team Against Urgencies	Hold Regular 1-on-1s
Day 21	**Day 22**	**Day 23**	**Day 24**	**Day 25**
Allow Others to Be Smart	Create Vision	Identify the Wildly Important Goals® (WIGs®)	Align Actions with the Wildly Important Goals	Ensure Your Systems Support Your Mission
Day 26	**Day 27**	**Day 28**	**Day 29**	**Day 30**
Deliver Results	Celebrate Wins	Make High-Value Decisions	Lead Through Change	Get Better

CHALLENGE 26

DELIVER RESULTS

Are you and your team delivering activities instead of results? Are the results the right ones?

Moving from a mess to success often requires a leader who supports and coaches you. I've benefited from a CEO who has been influencing me around one mess in particular: my focus. Not that I'm *not* focused on work and getting things done (quite the opposite); it's a matter of what happens when I execute on the things I'm focused on. I think the CEO would characterize it as "Scott can get anything done, but that's not always good."

> I'VE BENEFITED FROM A CEO WHO HAS BEEN INFLUENCING ME AROUND ONE MESS IN PARTICULAR: MY FOCUS. NOT THAT I'M NOT FOCUSED ON WORK AND GETTING THINGS DONE (QUITE THE OPPOSITE); IT'S A MATTER OF WHAT HAPPENS WHEN I EXECUTE ON THE THINGS I'M FOCUSED ON. I THINK THE CEO WOULD CHARACTERIZE IT AS "SCOTT CAN GET ANYTHING DONE, BUT THAT'S NOT ALWAYS GOOD."

Wait a minute! I'm sure you're thinking, *how is being able to get anything done not good?* Turns out, it goes something like this: Because I'm influential, know the organization inside and out, and have access to resources, I can easily divert many people's time and attention to "B" when, in reality, what matters most to the organization is "A." The fact is, it's not enough to get results; leaders must get the *right* results in the *right* way. "Right results" means what you're accomplishing is the right priority for the organization. It requires constantly recalibrating and checking in with your leader to make sure what you're working on is aligned to what your organization needs. And "right way" means getting the results in a way that won't burn out, injure, or demotivate your team. Leadership isn't about just running the current marathon, it's about that marathon and the next thirty and beyond.

There's a lesson we can draw from the world of horse racing. No one will dispute that horse racing is about getting results. It's a unique partnership between owner, trainer, jockey, and horse, all working together to win races. What you won't see, however, is a professional jockey riding a horse through an injury. It's an amazing sign of respect and love: jockeys will jump off midstream in a high-stakes race to stop and hold the horse's foot, protecting it from further injury. The *Toronto Sun* put it like this: "The first job of a jockey is to make sure the horse under him is running safe and sound. Then, if the horse is able to, try and win the race.... But if a jockey senses something just isn't right, abort the mission, no matter the circumstances." The writer was referencing the 2015 race when Mike Smith pulled up Shared Belief midway through the $1.5 million Charles Town Classic. There's no doubt that winning the big-money race was important to the owners of Shared Belief. But they understood that delivering results meant winning future races as well, and not just the one in front of them. To take the concept a step further, everyone around the horse knows that if the horse has an injury that prevents it from racing in the future, they put it out to stud (not an untenable alternative). If the injury is so severe the horse can't stand or walk, they may actually have to put it down (a tragic alternative).

It's too bad many leaders don't have the sense to treat their injured or struggling teams with as much care as jockeys do for an injured or struggling racehorse.

Now, let's shift our focus from how leaders treat their teams to how they get the right results. What's your reputation for getting results? Paraphrasing Henry Ford, "Nobody ever built a reputation on what they said they were going to do." Unless it's a reputation for *breaking* promises. It reminds me of an old Western where a gunslinger approached a cowboy at the bar. The cowboy, drink in hand, turned to the gunslinger and said, "You wouldn't want to shoot an unarmed man, would you? Just think what that would do to your reputation." The gunslinger responded without a moment's hesitation, "Yeah, but that *is* my reputation."

If you're a leader, you already have a reputation for driving results. The question is, what kind of reputation? One common mistake is for leaders to confuse activity with results. In fact, for several decades, being known for being "busy" was a coveted status. There was a tendency to equate "busy" with "productive." The busy worker was in demand; they were adding value. Multitasking was in vogue and often expressed as an actual competency.

In 2002, the *Harvard Business Review* published "Beware the Busy Manager." The article announced that leaders were paying a price for being overly busy. The authors found that 90 percent of managers squandered their time, while only 10 percent of managers spent their time in productive, committed, and reflective ways.

Today equating "busy" with "productive" has been debunked in all but the most antiquated of cultures. Busy is now decidedly uncool. FranklinCovey even produced an animated film titled Busy, Busy, Busy, featured in *The 7 Habits for Managers*® work session. It tells the story of a group of cartoon chickens metaphorically running around with their heads cut off and acting insanely busy—so busy, in fact, that the entire egg-generating enterprise collapses from fatigue. Circa 1997–2014, they could have cast me in the lead AND supporting roles, calling it *A Day in the Life of Scott Miller*. I promise you, if you watch the video, not only will you relate, but the song will possibly haunt you forever. Visit ManagementMess.com for some entertaining viewing.

Delivering results requires leaders to reject the belief that activity equals results; to affirm that, they deliver the *right* results by aligning their work to the mission and goals of the organization. Such leaders lead their teams with care and consideration so they achieve results in the *right* way. They are mindful of the health and welfare of their teams, so they win not just the current race, but the countless number of races ahead as well. And who knows, it may prevent the CEO from having to take time out of their busy day to rein you in (horse pun intended).

FROM MESS TO SUCCESS:
DELIVER RESULTS

- Have you assessed whether the results you're achieving are the same results your leader expects? It's great to overdeliver with additional projects, but they cannot come at the expense of your core responsibilities or business goals.

- Take the initiative and proactively check in with your leader to ensure you're properly aligned and focused on the right priorities. Goals shift, and you may not always be aware of that in real time.

- Don't hesitate to seek a reality check about your performance. Don't assume your results speak for themselves; you may need to highlight them or course-correct, based on the feedback you receive.

- Thoughtfully calibrate the pressure you place on your teams to ensure you are achieving results now in ways that will allow you to achieve them again in the future.

- Remember to coach to results, not activity.

Day 1	Day 2	Day 3	Day 4	Day 5
Demonstrate Humility	Think Abundantly	Listen First	Declare Your Intent	Make and Keep Commitments
Day 6	**Day 7**	**Day 8**	**Day 9**	**Day 10**
Carry Your Own Weather	Inspire Trust	Model Work/Life Balance	Place the Right People in the Right Roles	Make Time for Relationships
Day 11	**Day 12**	**Day 13**	**Day 14**	**Day 15**
Check Your Paradigms	Lead Difficult Conversations	Talk Straight	Balance Courage and Consideration	Show Loyalty
Day 16	**Day 17**	**Day 18**	**Day 19**	**Day 20**
Make It Safe to Tell the Truth	Right Wrongs	Coach Continuously	Protect Your Team Against Urgencies	Hold Regular 1-on-1s
Day 21	**Day 22**	**Day 23**	**Day 24**	**Day 25**
Allow Others to Be Smart	Create Vision	Identify the Wildly Important Goals® (WIGs®)	Align Actions with the Wildly Important Goals	Ensure Your Systems Support Your Mission
Day 26	**Day 27**	**Day 28**	**Day 29**	**Day 30**
Deliver Results	Celebrate Wins	Make High-Value Decisions	Lead Through Change	Get Better

CHALLENGE 27

CELEBRATE WINS

Do you spend as much time celebrating the
achievement of goals as you do setting them?

Recently, I had an idea to celebrate a big win in a big way. I was leading a session with a number of business leaders from around the world—*very* successful individuals, many of whom had led significant careers prior to their partnership representing FranklinCovey's solutions in their respective home countries.

> ...BUDGET SHOULD NEVER CONSTRAIN YOUR ABILITY TO CELEBRATE WINS. PEOPLE MIGHT BE HAPPY TO GET SOME FREE FOOD OR GIFTS OUT OF A CELEBRATORY EVENT, BUT I PROMISE, IF YOU INVEST TIME IN RECOGNIZING THEM, YOU CAN MAKE A BIGGER, MORE LASTING IMPRESSION. WHAT DOESN'T COST YOU ANY FUNDS? SPEND AN HOUR THE NIGHT BEFORE AND GENERATE A LIST OF EACH PERSON'S UNIQUE CONTRIBUTIONS TO A BIG WIN. IN FACT, I'D ENCOURAGE YOU TO MEMORIZE IT. THE NEXT DAY, GO ONE BY ONE AROUND THE ROOM AND SHARE.

My goal was to celebrate the success they'd had in building their prospecting databases, and also take a quantum leap in the number of people they could add to their target audience. You see, I wanted to celebrate their current successes and share a vision of what was possible.

So, did I plan a black-tie affair with a quintet playing Bach? No. Fancy wine and cheese? Nope. I had the staff wheeling three confetti cannons toward the intimate gathering as I shared statistics regarding potential prospects in each country: a few hundred thousand here, a million or so there, totaling twenty-eight million potential prospects across our collective databases. It's an impressive number to talk about. It's an even more impressive number to experience. On command, the cannons were set off. Suddenly, the air filled with twenty-eight million pieces of confetti.

Otherwise buttoned-down executives jumped up from their seats, many pulling out cellphones and capturing it on video, while others started dancing and laughing, celebrating to the synchronized music in the background. At one point, I even passed out umbrellas as the confetti showers continued. (My apologies to the hotel cleaning staff, who are probably still cursing my name to this day.) For your viewing pleasure, visit www.ManagementMess.com for some clips of this celebration.

Sure, Scott, that's fine when you have the budget for cannons and confetti, you might say to yourself, *but I don't.* I hear you, but this is important: Budget should NEVER constrain your ability to celebrate wins. People might be happy to get some free food or gifts out of a celebratory event, but I promise if you invest time in recognizing them, you can make a bigger, more lasting impression. What doesn't cost you any funds? Spend an hour the night before and generate a list of each person's unique contributions to a big win. In fact, I'd encourage you to memorize it. The next day, go one by one around the room and share. I promise it's something your team members are likely to never forget. I believe in this practice so much that I memorized all the names, faces, and backgrounds of each of the attendees at the rehearsal dinner prior to our wedding. I walked around the room, named every person at the reception, and pointed out a little about them and what they meant to my fiancée and me. Certainly, the least expensive (by a long stretch) activity of the wedding. But memorable? Absolutely.

As a leader, remember that people like to win, but not "fake" win. Your team wants to work for it. But they don't want the finish line moved, and they don't want to kill themselves in the process. And when it's over, they want to celebrate the victory. What can keep that from happening? For one, being a perfectionist.

Perfectionists set goals that are absurdly high and crush the spirits and hopes of those they've enlisted to achieve them. They recruit willing, competent people to follow them in what I call *chasing the leprechaun*. If you think you'll win that pot of gold in the end, you're crazy.

I, like most people, desire some perfection in my life—from my mechanic, elevator engineer, surgeon, and eventually my embalmer—but that desire must be tempered in a leadership role. If you're a perfectionist, define what "extraordinary" looks like (not "perfect"), and take pride when you and your team achieve it. Just because you feel you aren't winning by an impossible definition of success doesn't mean you aren't winning.

Leaders must also fight the compulsion to wait for just the right "special occasion" to celebrate. Back when people watched actual television sets weighing north of a hundred pounds with only three channels and a coat hanger turned antenna, *Good Morning America* had a recurring guest named Erma Bombeck. She was a wife, mother, journalist, and truth-teller. She was magical, and today her books remain among my favorite reads. (Must-buys are *The Grass Is Always Greener Over the Septic Tank* and *When You Look Like Your Passport Photo, It's Time to Go Home*.) One of the most indelible memories bestowed by Erma was an anecdote referring to our tendency to save, cherish, and never use the fine china, our keepsakes, photo albums, etc. She wisely admitted, "I would have burned the pink candle that was sculpted like a rose before it melted while being stored."

Erma inspired me to use up and enjoy everything I own. Case in point, my father-in-law recently gave me a vintage bottle of champagne from his personal collection. It included a note to "save it for a very special day." The next week, he sold a long-listed property, so I popped the cork. It irritated my father-in-law, but I use stuff up with joy at every chance.

What resources do you have as a leader that are wasting away? My advice is to burn that rose-sculpted candle. Don't hold back celebrating wins for just "very special days." On the flip side, don't celebrate every accomplishment, because you'll lose credibility and nothing becomes noteworthy. Find legitimate reasons to celebrate and be generous with your "stuff." If you have a discretionary budget, spend it. Most important of all, use the time you have to invest in recognizing your team's accomplishments. And if you have access to confetti cannons, they work great too.

FROM MESS TO SUCCESS:
CELEBRATE WINS

- Understand your culture's propensity to celebrate: Is it enough? not enough? too much?

- Assess your people's ability to actually "win." Are your goals so lofty that they have an inverse impact and crush people's spirits?

- Plan your team's next celebration:

  1. What contributions should be recognized?
  2. Outline what you intend to say about each team member. Be specific.

- Identify an appropriate reward to share with the individual or team. Customize it to the recipient's preferences and the project's scope.

Day 1	Day 2	Day 3	Day 4	Day 5
Demonstrate Humility	Think Abundantly	Listen First	Declare Your Intent	Make and Keep Commitments
Day 6	**Day 7**	**Day 8**	**Day 9**	**Day 10**
Carry Your Own Weather	Inspire Trust	Model Work/Life Balance	Place the Right People in the Right Roles	Make Time for Relationships
Day 11	**Day 12**	**Day 13**	**Day 14**	**Day 15**
Check Your Paradigms	Lead Difficult Conversations	Talk Straight	Balance Courage and Consideration	Show Loyalty
Day 16	**Day 17**	**Day 18**	**Day 19**	**Day 20**
Make It Safe to Tell the Truth	Right Wrongs	Coach Continuously	Protect Your Team Against Urgencies	Hold Regular 1-on-1s
Day 21	**Day 22**	**Day 23**	**Day 24**	**Day 25**
Allow Others to Be Smart	Create Vision	Identify the Wildly Important Goals® (WIGs®)	Align Actions with the Wildly Important Goals	Ensure Your Systems Support Your Mission
Day 26	**Day 27**	**Day 28**	**Day 29**	**Day 30**
Deliver Results	Celebrate Wins	Make High-Value Decisions	Lead Through Change	Get Better

CHALLENGE 28

MAKE HIGH-VALUE DECISIONS

Do you dedicate your time to the activities that will yield the most impactful results on the organization and your team's mission?

As a leader, your reputation is, in essence, the sum of your collective decisions. Basically, you're paid to decide—it's that simple. You likely make hundreds of decisions every week, some insignificant and others so impactful they could change the course of your entire organization. Leaders decide:

- Who to hire and who to fire.

- What to elevate as a priority and what to push aside.

- What to celebrate and what to ignore.

- What gets funded and what gets starved.

I'VE COME TO THINK OF HIGH-VALUE DECISIONS AS THE ACTIONS THAT BRING DISPROPORTIONATE PROGRESS TOWARD THE ORGANIZATION'S MISSION, VISION, AND WIGS. IT MIGHT BE SOMETHING CLIENT-FOCUSED, COST-FOCUSED, PERFORMANCE-FOCUSED, INNOVATION-FOCUSED... THE OPTIONS ARE LIMITLESS. AND THEREIN LIES THE CHALLENGE. IF YOU'RE LOOKING TO MOVE FROM MESS TO SUCCESS IN THIS REGARD, ASSESS HOW YOU SPEND YOUR TIME, EVEN ON A DAILY AND HOURLY BASIS. ASK YOURSELF, "IS WHAT I AM DOING NOW, OR WHAT I AM GOING TO DO NEXT, PROGRESSING OUR MISSION AND VISION OR OUR WILDLY IMPORTANT GOALS?"

Making such decisions involves carrying a lot of responsibility. I've seen very competent, well-respected people with admirable work ethics and high character make decisions that cost their organizations millions of wasted dollars and irreparably injured their careers. I struggled with this early in my career. I didn't waste millions of dollars, but I'm certain my reputation took a hit.

After a successful tenure running the company's largest sales region from Chicago, I accepted a position at the company headquarters in Salt Lake City. When you get feedback as a sales leader, it's quick and never wrong—you either hit your number or you didn't. When I arrived at my new office in Utah, I had a swagger, an inflated ego, and believed I could do no wrong. Who wouldn't be excited to work with this level of management mess, right?

My new job involved expanding the client-facilitator channel for the organization—no more revenue spreadsheets with my name on them. Since I was the first person in the role, there were no previous failures or successes to be measured against. It was as "blue ocean" an opportunity as I ever had up to that point in my career. Each workday amounted to endless opportunities, prompting a countless number of possible decisions. With an office just down the hall from the CEO and uncharted territory for me to explore and build, this should have been a slam-dunk, hole-in-one, I-just-stretched-my-t-shirt-in-a-bicep-curl kind of moment.

Only it wasn't.

Without the constant feedback and tension of revenue goals, I struggled to prioritize my time. I focused on projects that made *me* feel good and validated my own biases on what needed to be accomplished but weren't likely of the highest value to the company. No one would say I was wasting resources or being irrelevant—I was working harder than ever. But what I was working on wouldn't have been viewed by the CEO as the most important areas of focus. Without the benefit of the mutual, robust collaboration I had grown accustomed to in Chicago, I made many decisions on my own, few of which I'd categorize as high-value.

I've come to think of high-value decisions as the actions that bring disproportionate progress toward the organization's mission, vision, and WIGs. It might be something client-focused, cost-focused, performance-focused, innovation-focused... the options are limitless. And therein lies the challenge. If you're looking to move from mess to success in this regard, assess how you spend your time, even on a daily and an hourly basis. Ask yourself, "Is what I am doing now, or what I am going to do next, progressing our mission and vision or our Wildly Important Goals?" In *The 5 Choices: The Path to Extraordinary Productivity*, the authors write that high-value decisions result from:

- Working on the important, not the urgent—going for the extraordinary, not the ordinary.

- Focusing one's attention on the right things—how leaders prioritize and manage their time.

- Having sustained energy. Leaders who burn out and don't renew their energy won't have the capacity to recognize and drive high-value decisions to completion.

In addition, I've discerned that making high-value decisions requires first admitting that it's okay if you don't have the answer. Help build the kind of trust with your leader that allows you to share what you're working on and get input on how to organize and prioritize your time. I have three "lessons learned" from my experience with high-value decisions:

- Focus. With unlimited choices comes the temptation to take on those that don't meet the high-value criteria. The fact that I *could* fly to 190 countries didn't mean that I *should*. With better focus, I could have found better ways to spend my time.

- Don't go it alone. If you're stuck, feeling disenfranchised, or just can't decide between two compelling but incompatible choices, get help. Humbly share your ideas with a leader and ask for guidance. Asking, "What's the best use of my time, talents, and budget?" can bring much-needed insights and direction.

- Don't go for the easy wins. There's a reason *The 5 Choices* authors urge us to go for the extraordinary and not the ordinary. As leaders, we may be tempted to play to our strengths, find the path of least resistance, and go for the easy wins that will bring recognition and reward. But rarely is that the path that leads to high-value decisions.

Do something important but hard—stretch yourself and keep your energy and drive high.

I've also seen numerous leaders fail to make high-value decisions. Consider whether you might be prone to one or more of these management messes:

- You have a "go it alone" personality. As a result, you risk not getting the input from others that the train isn't just off the tracks, but headed off the bridge into the river.

- You're so buried in projects, you can't see a way forward (or even recognize how deep you're in).

- You know you need help and you're tempted to involve others, but you lack the humility and/or courage to engage someone with deeper expertise.

- You shy away from solving problems that feel awkward or uncomfortable, such as holding a high-courage performance conversation.

- You haven't developed the discipline to ask, "What am I going to do today to bring extraordinary value to my organization? Are there things I should say no to that are getting in the way?"

- You've allowed yourself to get sucked into the vortex of unlimited choices.

- You've filled your days with meetings and calls that are part of someone else's agenda.

- You've failed to be hyper-intentional about how you spend your time, attention, and decision-making capacity.

The challenges in this book are a pathway for action—a blueprint to build your unique leadership on. Accept the responsibility to make high-value decisions and watch your contribution, reputation, and brand explode.

FROM MESS TO SUCCESS:
MAKE HIGH-VALUE DECISIONS

- Remember, your reputation is the totality of your decisions, not only in your professional life, but also in your personal life. In fact, your whole life.

- Use the bulleted "messes" above as an assessment. What will you work on?

- Go for the extraordinary. High-value decisions are rarely grounded in the ordinary.

- Regularly challenge your decision making to determine whether it should be elevated. Shouldn't your decision-making capacity improve each week? What are you doing to assess the outcomes of your previous decisions and surpass them going forward?

Day 1	Day 2	Day 3	Day 4	Day 5
Demonstrate Humility	Think Abundantly	Listen First	Declare Your Intent	Make and Keep Commitments
Day 6	**Day 7**	**Day 8**	**Day 9**	**Day 10**
Carry Your Own Weather	Inspire Trust	Model Work/Life Balance	Place the Right People in the Right Roles	Make Time for Relationships
Day 11	**Day 12**	**Day 13**	**Day 14**	**Day 15**
Check Your Paradigms	Lead Difficult Conversations	Talk Straight	Balance Courage and Consideration	Show Loyalty
Day 16	**Day 17**	**Day 18**	**Day 19**	**Day 20**
Make It Safe to Tell the Truth	Right Wrongs	Coach Continuously	Protect Your Team Against Urgencies	Hold Regular 1-on-1s
Day 21	**Day 22**	**Day 23**	**Day 24**	**Day 25**
Allow Others to Be Smart	Create Vision	Identify the Wildly Important Goals® (WIGs®)	Align Actions with the Wildly Important Goals	Ensure Your Systems Support Your Mission
Day 26	**Day 27**	**Day 28**	**Day 29**	**Day 30**
Deliver Results	Celebrate Wins	Make High-Value Decisions	Lead Through Change	Get Better

CHALLENGE 29

LEAD THROUGH CHANGE

When leading change, are you calm, confident, and focused—or anxious, threatened, and scattered?

Change comes at us nonstop in every form: organizational structures, market competition, government regulations, tax laws, revenue expectations, financial and accounting requirements, quality initiatives, unexpected events… it's unrelenting. For the purpose of this challenge, I've decided to write through the particular lens of changes with people—where it tends to get the messiest and most personal. Hang on for the ride, it's going to be raw.

Isn't the whole point of leadership to effect positive change? I mean, nobody is paying us to secure the status quo. And as it relates specifically to leading others, shouldn't the ultimate change manifest as you watch someone you've coached and invested in succeed? My personal experience around this indicates yes… *apparently, though, just as long as they don't surpass me*. That seems to be my limit.

ISN'T THE WHOLE POINT OF LEADERSHIP TO EFFECT POSITIVE CHANGE? I MEAN, NOBODY IS PAYING US TO SECURE THE STATUS QUO. AND AS IT RELATES SPECIFICALLY TO LEADING OTHERS, SHOULDN'T THE ULTIMATE CHANGE MANIFEST AS YOU WATCH SOMEONE YOU'VE COACHED AND INVESTED IN SUCCEED?

It's insights like this that prompted my editor to call aspects of my leadership career a "management mess." It came quickly (maybe a little too quickly) as titles for this book were being bounced around. And here's the irony: While on this sometimes messy journey, I've consistently been recognized as someone who deliberately invests in others.

I take great joy in seeing those around me earn promotions, increase their incomes, and grow their influence. I could count dozens of people who have gone on to fantastic careers after I was privileged to be their leader for some time. I'd like to think I had a small role in setting them up for their future successes. But sadly, as I've admitted above, there's a caveat to my self-congratulatory tone: I love seeing you change and succeed, so long as it's not more than me. You'll be pleased to know I'm currently rereading Challenge 2 (Think Abundantly) for my own professional development.

Case in point: There's a colleague of mine whom I've worked with for fifteen-plus years. I've often said to Paul that he's the younger brother I *never* had but *always* wanted, and I'm the older brother he *never* had and *never* wanted. He's followed my path closely, even filling roles I'd left, each time improving on my performance and legacy. In hindsight, I felt comfortable with his success; proud of it, in fact, even when his performance in those roles always seemed to eclipse mine. I was truly delighted with his wins, and this continued for many years. He is smart, trustworthy, hardworking, disciplined, and has grown his maturity and skillsets substantially. That seemed validating to me, as he and others have acknowledged my investment in him over the years.

Then it finally happened—honestly, I knew it was coming—the CEO elevated Paul. Above me.

It was only a matter of time before he earned the promotion, a decision I solidly endorsed on the executive team. Then reality began to set in, and for reasons I'm still discerning, it was a bit much for me to digest. (Isn't it remarkable how change can make logical sense, yet we still struggle with it emotionally?) My challenge is ongoing because, oddly, I don't want the job he has, I'm not qualified for it, and I don't want to get qualified for it. In my ongoing introspection, I'm sensing that my reaction was due to it being the first time in my career that I'd watched someone progress not just up to my level, but past it. It's truly zero percent about Paul and a hundred percent about me. To be clear, to those of you growing increasingly uncomfortable (I warned you about it being raw), I think he's unequivocally the right person for the role. Our entire firm, clients, and shareholders will benefit from his promotion.

As a result of my shared reflection, I assume one of two things will happen: a percentage of you will send me supportive emails and tweets about how relatable and vulnerable I am (success); the other percentage will send vitriolic emails and tweets challenging my ability to even hold a leadership role at my level (mess).

I think it proves the adage that people support change when it's their idea and don't when it's not. Or in my case, I support it when it impacts *you*, but less so when it impacts *me*.

The announcement of Paul's promotion was made to the immediate leadership team, and I just couldn't keep my jealousy at bay. When I returned to my team of directors to discuss the decision, I feigned excitement; then I promptly told everyone that I supported the decision but would not be reporting to Paul—and likely never would. I conveyed my belief that he was right for the role and that I expected them to support it. Anyone with half a brain could have read my mind and discerned my tepid support.

How pitiful—and, candidly, inappropriate. I must have looked petty and foolish to my team.

A colleague called me out. On the spot. Strongly.

I deflected the criticism with some classic Scott-level indignation and began to talk about how the new organizational structure might impact the team and how we would move forward. To my team's credit, several of them asked me how I was feeling about the decision, and even went so far as to validate my real-time struggle. (They were still encouraged about the leadership change, however.)

Each of us will have our own triggers around change. I've openly shared mine (and hopefully you have a good therapist for sharing yours). The truth is that most people believe change will make things worse for them, not better. According to Alan Deutschman in *Change or Die*, 88 percent of us take on a pessimistic outlook with change. In FranklinCovey's offering designed for first-level leaders *The 6 Critical Practices for Leading a Team*, leaders confront this dilemma by first adopting a new mindset—moving from trying to control and contain change to championing it. As I look back, it's easy to see how my fear and attempts at control and containment negatively impacted both my brand and my credibility, traits I had worked enormously hard to build for years.

The emotional impact organizational change has on your team must not be underestimated. As a leader, you most likely were part of the inside conversation. You may well have context for all the discussion and debate that led up to the ultimate decision. As a result, you may not have recognized the value of time spent in reconciling and understanding the change yourself.

Consider these practices I've found useful for leading through change:

- Recognize how the change impacts you. How you relate to and experience it will impact how you communicate it to others. Don't short-circuit your own needs to process and understand the change; you deserve to work through the process to ensure you can communicate and promote the news. You may need to even tell yourself, "I need to check my own opinions as I continue to digest, understand, and own this change."

- Ask as many questions as possible to ensure you can shape the context for your own team. The more you know and understand, the better you can lead them through the process.

- Identify the level of transparency. Be intentional about what you disclose to ensure your team can process the change at the speed they need to. Sometimes you don't have the luxury of time on your side, and every situation may require a tailored approach. What is consistent is that people can generally handle tough news. What they won't tolerate is the wrong news or no news. Do your level best to share what you know, acknowledge what you don't, and commit to keeping everyone informed as promptly and consistently as is reasonable.

- Decide what your communication style will be during the change. You may need to balance your own mixed feelings while honoring your professional responsibility.

You'll learn to lead through change by putting some space between the news you receive (the stimulus) and how you react (your response). You may need to put your personal emotions aside for the time being, even compartmentalize them, while you plan how you're going to champion the change for the benefit of the organization. This particular management mess is one I'm still tangled up in, but I'm working toward turning it into an eventual leadership success.

For the record, Paul, I'm proud of you.

FROM MESS TO SUCCESS:
LEAD THROUGH CHANGE

- Recognize that change and growth is hard. It's okay to struggle with it. The fact that you're a leader doesn't mean you're immune to having emotional reactions to change. Allow yourself to work through a process. But be judicious about doing it privately versus publicly.

- Consider separating how the change impacts you personally from its effect on the organization. Focus on what you can champion as you marshal the change for the benefit of others. Your team members are watching you carefully for how you project confidence and regulate your emotions. The more mindful you are of this truth, the better you can model what you want to see from them.

- Remember to think abundantly (Challenge 2). Change often opens new doors, experiences, opportunities, etc.

Day 1	Day 2	Day 3	Day 4	Day 5
Demonstrate Humility	Think Abundantly	Listen First	Declare Your Intent	Make and Keep Commitments
Day 6	**Day 7**	**Day 8**	**Day 9**	**Day 10**
Carry Your Own Weather	Inspire Trust	Model Work /Life Balance	Place the Right People in the Right Roles	Make Time for Relationships
Day 11	**Day 12**	**Day 13**	**Day 14**	**Day 15**
Check Your Paradigms	Lead Difficult Conversations	Talk Straight	Balance Courage and Consideration	Show Loyalty
Day 16	**Day 17**	**Day 18**	**Day 19**	**Day 20**
Make It Safe to Tell the Truth	Right Wrongs	Coach Continuously	Protect Your Team Against Urgencies	Hold Regular 1-on-1s
Day 21	**Day 22**	**Day 23**	**Day 24**	**Day 25**
Allow Others to Be Smart	Create Vision	Identify the Wildly Important Goals® (WIGs®)	Align Actions with the Wildly Important Goals	Ensure Your Systems Support Your Mission
Day 26	**Day 27**	**Day 28**	**Day 29**	**Day 30**
Deliver Results	Celebrate Wins	Make High-Value Decisions	Lead Through Change	Get Better

CHALLENGE 30

GET BETTER

Are you consistently assessing
your relevance and advancing
your skills and capabilities?

This challenge isn't about making incremental improvements in your professional development, relevance, or competencies. I challenge you to not just double down, but to quadruple down. And when you do, you will stand out and secure your relevance and write your future.

I have a deep interest in people's professional journeys. In the *On Leadership* series I host, we invite renowned thought leaders, bestselling authors, and recognized industry experts to join for a weekly conversation on their areas of excellence. Personally, I learn so much each week, I can't possibly digest it all at once. I ask every guest the same general question in the opening, which is to describe their path: What led them to their success? Two commonalities exist among nearly all of my guests.

- An unyielding, insatiable curiosity about a particular topic.

- A relentless drive to understand and then communicate it better than anyone else on the planet.

Something else these industry experts and thought leaders all absolutely have in common, which they'd rarely admit in public, is that they continually disrupt/reinvent themselves. They're ahead of the curve, the downturn, and their own eventual boredom with their last topic.

THIS CHALLENGE ISN'T ABOUT MAKING INCREMENTAL IMPROVEMENTS IN YOUR PROFESSIONAL DEVELOPMENT, RELEVANCE, OR COMPETENCIES. I CHALLENGE YOU TO NOT JUST DOUBLE DOWN BUT TO QUADRUPLE DOWN.

Malcolm Gladwell, whom I've not interviewed (yet), never rests on his last success. His books, speeches, and articles cover unexpectedly fresh topics I'd never think to associate him with, so that he's constantly surprising me with his evolving areas of interest and focus. Malcolm is a superb example for all of us trying to stay ahead, remain relevant, and become indispensable. This is a personal challenge I've taken to heart my entire career, and something I hold as a core strength. But not without some missteps along the way. This crystallized for me one day while I was chatting with the renowned marketing authority Seth Godin. He reminded me of the value of knowing the difference between being reckless and being fearless.

Drop the mic.

I've shared this distinction with others countless times as it relates to our own leadership journeys. In my case, I spent too many years thinking I was fearless when I was, in fact, being reckless (as this book highlights). Now I am crystal clear on the differences, and I'm intent on becoming fearless, at least with my career. So no raw oysters or grappa for me!

Being reckless means taking actions that could irreparably injure your brand, reputation, or even the self-esteem or feelings of another person. Being fearless, however, is taking thoughtful risks where the payoff can be enormous, but the downside (failure) is manageable and likely only impacts you. Quitting your job to write the great American novel with no agent, publisher, or savings account is being reckless. Picking up the phone and pitching your idea to every editor you can find and being emboldened by the naïveté of those imbeciles who reject you is being fearless (just ask J. K. Rowling).

Yes, I have fears—no skydiving, bungee-jumping, or scuba-diving events in my calendar. But professionally, I am fearless enough to take on anything, and it has served me immensely well. To be clear, I don't jump into things without preparation and awareness. I know my strengths and how far I can push them. And typically, that means going past my comfort level or what others think I'm capable of. I jump into things and work my ass off to ensure a win. And I recruit as many competent people as I can to join me along the way. I think this drive and willingness to "put myself out there" has paid vast dividends to my career. I also, to be honest, have learned to discern whose feedback I care about and whose I don't. No surprise, there's a group of people who don't care for me. Frankly, I don't even think about them. I crave the feedback and advice of those who I am assured have my best interests in mind.

What's the point of my prior diatribe about being reckless versus fearless? I passionately encourage you to be fearless about your own professional development and learning. Make quantum leaps. What's the standard old-school advice for this? Listening to podcasts, attending industry conferences, reading academic literature, watching TED Talks, blah, blah, blah… kill me, please.

Take risks. Produce your own podcast; host your own internal company conference; write your own damn article; stop watching TED Talks and record your own instead. Get out there and rebrand yourself through new skills supporting new ambitions.

The best tactical advice for getting better comes from *The Speed of Trust*. Tips for getting better:

- Commit to continuous improvement. If you haven't made the mental decision to strive for improvement in a specific area, you'll live contently in the status quo. This book offers you thirty challenges to do the former—instead of putting the book down once you've finished it, schedule specific challenges in your calendar.

- Increase your capabilities. Until we live in some utopian future where we can plug our minds (and biceps) into a machine and magically grow them, the only way to make gains is to stretch ourselves, do hard things, fail, learn, grow, succeed, and repeat.

- Be a constant learner. The fact that you're reading this book proves you have the drive to learn and reinvent yourself. Keep it up! Never assume the knowledge and skills you have today will be sufficient for the challenges of tomorrow.

- Develop feedback systems. Believe it or not, without feedback, our well-intentioned efforts to get better can languish and even backfire. How do you know you're making gains in important areas, or for that matter, the right areas? Put feedback mechanisms in place and make it safe for others to tell you the truth (see Challenge 16).

- Act upon the feedback you receive. Many of the challenges in this book will help you put feedback into action, such as Challenge 5: Make and Keep Commitments. Translate feedback into specific behaviors your team can see you doing.

A final thought on feedback: I'm not interested in *everyone's* opinion. And I don't think you should be either. When you work to get better, you're putting yourself out there. The world is full of naysayers, pessimists, critics, and those who are forever content to stay on the sidelines. So I'll end with a quote from Brené Brown's book *Rising Strong*. I read it daily. It's my new mantra for building my skills, taking risks, and learning, trying, failing, and trying again—you know, getting better:

"A lot of cheap seats in the arena are filled with people who never venture onto the floor. They just hurl mean-spirited

I PASSIONATELY ENCOURAGE YOU TO BE FEARLESS ABOUT YOUR OWN PROFESSIONAL DEVELOPMENT AND LEARNING. MAKE QUANTUM LEAPS. WHAT'S THE STANDARD OLD-SCHOOL ADVICE FOR THIS? LISTENING TO PODCASTS, ATTENDING INDUSTRY CONFERENCES, READING ACADEMIC LITERATURE, WATCHING TED TALKS, BLAH, BLAH, BLAH... KILL ME, PLEASE.

TAKE RISKS. PRODUCE YOUR OWN PODCAST; HOST YOUR OWN INTERNAL COMPANY CONFERENCE; WRITE YOUR OWN DAMN ARTICLE; STOP WATCHING TED TALKS AND RECORD YOUR OWN INSTEAD. GET OUT THERE AND REBRAND YOURSELF THROUGH NEW SKILLS SUPPORTING NEW AMBITIONS.

criticisms and put-downs from a safe distance. The problem is, when we stop caring what people think and stop feeling hurt by cruelty, we lose our ability to connect. But when we're defined by what people think, we lose the courage to be vulnerable. Therefore, we need to be selective about the feedback we let into our lives. For me, if you're not in the arena getting your ass kicked, I'm not interested in your feedback."

So go out there, jump into the leadership arena, and put the thirty challenges into practice. And when you inevitably find you're getting your *derriere* kicked, keep in mind the various messes and successes I've experienced (or caused) over the years. And know that with every well-delivered kick came an insight, a course correction, a relationship epiphany, a desire to pick myself up, recommit, and get better. I invite you to join me on the field, not be embarrassed by the bumps and bruises collected along the way, and engage in that most noble, life-changing, and potentially world-changing endeavor: to be a leader.

FROM MESS TO SUCCESS:
GET BETTER

- Assign each of the thirty challenges a day on your calendar. Prioritize them according to where you feel, or others have indicated, you could benefit most.

- Identify those challenges where your confidence is high and congratulate yourself. Be proud of it! Ask yourself: "As a current strength, could some refinement even make it my 'killer app'?"

- You've got enough stuff to work on by this point. I'm not assigning you any more prompts. Go have a beer and think about what's next on your leadership journey.

FROM MESS TO SUCCESS:
GET BETTER BONUS

(a.k.a. Scott's List of Gratuitous Self-Promotional Activities)

As the Executive Vice President of Thought Leadership for FranklinCovey, I am privileged to engage with three different leadership-development opportunities. The first consists of a weekday, less than one-minute, leadership insight I've gleaned from over twenty-five years in the industry, and can be seen on any of my social channels:

- Facebook: https://www.facebook.com/ScottMillerFC/

- Twitter: https://twitter.com/ScottMillerFC

- LinkedIn: https://www.linkedin.com/in/scottmillerfc/

- Instagram: https://www.instagram.com/scottmillerfc/

Second, I host a weekly radio program on iHeartRadio titled *Great Life, Great Career With Scott Miller.* This hour-long interview program delves into practical leadership advice given by various bestselling authors, industry titans, and regular people like you and me who have incredible stories and experiences to share. Join me here:

- https://www.iheart.com/podcast/420-great-life-great-career-sc-30164198/episodes/

- https://itunes.apple.com/us/podcast/great-life-great-career/id1438915013?mt=2

- https://www.stitcher.com/podcast/franklincovey/great-life-great-career

- https://resources.franklincovey.com/greatlifegreatcareer

- https://soundcloud.com/great-life-great-career

Third, I have the honor of hosting a program for FranklinCovey titled *On Leadership With Scott Miller.* This weekly newsletter features compelling interviews with bestselling authors, renowned authorities, speakers, and public figures to discuss their unique perspectives on leadership. What sets *On Leadership With Scott Miller* apart is that it is now the world's fastest-growing weekly newsletter dedicated to leadership development. Completely complimentary from FranklinCovey, it consists of the featured interview, a blog post, and a downloadable tool that will help you and your team members immediately implement the insights. I encourage you to subscribe at:

- http://resources.franklincovey.com/on-leadership

WHAT ABOUT CHARACTER?

I suspect some of you may be wondering why certain leadership competencies you're passionate about, or that FranklinCovey teaches, weren't included in this book. When my colleagues and I worked to narrow down the list, we left dozens of them off, mainly to keep the challenges and book manageable (and you're thinking: *thirty is manageable?*). It could easily have become overwhelming if we'd added in every leadership principle, competency, or challenge you'll ever face. As you can tell, I like digestibility. Small, actionable insights I can remember and try to integrate into my life immediately.

There is one foundational challenge, more critical than anything else, not included here: character. For those readers who are familiar with FranklinCovey's legacy and reputation, our other books, solutions, and overall approach to effectiveness, you know that at the core of everything we believe and teach is the value of both your character and your competence. This book focuses mainly on your competence: your beliefs, actions, and even reactions. It's mainly dedicated to behaviors, some of which I suspect you've already thought about working on as a specific challenge spoke to you.

I didn't intentionally leave character out. To quote Joel Peterson, Stanford Graduate School of Business professor and chairman of JetBlue Airways, "Character is your ticket to the game." Your character is your foundation. It's the basis for who you are in every aspect of your life—as a leader, parent, spouse, friend, partner, or colleague.

Look at those leaders and teachers who have lasting, enduring impact in our lives. It's typically their character that either sustains their reputation or destroys it. Every day it seems we're faced with another example of people we might follow, admire, and respect, who undermine their own influence and legacies through lapses in their character. Built over decades, destroyed in minutes.

Don't confuse or correlate the decision not to include character in this book with its unimportance. Let me be clear. None of these leadership challenges matter if you fail on the character challenge. And they are, in fact, mostly presented to you as challenges, issues you face sometimes on an hourly basis. Most are clear and matter-of-fact issues that actually test or confirm your character. Those are (or should be) the easy ones. The stuff people around you see is fairly easy to make the right call on. It's the others, the more nuanced opportunities, that may seem small or insignificant in the moment, that are disproportionately valuable in reinforcing your character. The hidden stuff. The behaviors nobody sees—perhaps ever. In fact, in many cases, only one person will. You.

CHALLENGE SOURCES

LEAD YOURSELF

1. Demonstrate Humility—*Leading at the Speed of Trust*

2. Think Abundantly—*The 7 Habits of Highly Effective People*

3. Listen First—*The 7 Habits of Highly Effective People; The Speed of Trust*

4. Declare Your Intent—*Leading at the Speed of Trust*

5. Make and Keep Commitments—*Speed of Trust Foundations*

6. Carry Your Own Weather—*The 7 Habits of Highly Effective People*

7. Inspire Trust—*Leading at the Speed of Trust*

8. Model Work/Life Balance—*The 5 Choices to Extraordinary Productivity*

LEAD OTHERS

9. Place the Right People in the Right Roles—*The 4 Essential Roles of Leadership*

10. Make Time for Relationships—*The 4 Essential Roles of Leadership*

11. Check Your Paradigms—*The 7 Habits of Highly Effective People*

12. Lead Difficult Conversations—*The 4 Essential Roles of Leadership*

13. Talk Straight—*Leading at the Speed of Trust*

14. Balance Courage and Consideration—*The 7 Habits of Highly Effective People*

15. Show Loyalty—*Leading at the Speed of Trust Foundations*

16. Make It Safe to Tell the Truth—*Get Better: 15 Proven Practices to Building Effective Relationships at Work*

17. Right Wrongs—*Leading at the Speed of Trust*

18. Coach Continuously—*The 4 Essential Roles of Leadership*

19. Protect Your Team Against Urgencies—*The 5 Choices to Extraordinary Productivity*

20. Hold Regular 1-on-1s—*The 6 Critical Practices for Leading a Team*

21. Allow Others to Be Smart—*The 4 Essential Roles of Leadership*

GET RESULTS

22. Create Vision—*The 4 Essential Roles of Leadership*

23. Identify the Wildly Important Goals—*The 4 Disciplines of Execution*

24. Align Actions With the Wildly Important Goals—*The 4 Disciplines of Execution*

25. Ensure Your Systems Support Your Mission—*The 4 Essential Roles of Leadership*

26. Deliver Results—*Leading at the Speed of Trust*

27. Celebrate Wins—*Project Management Essentials for the Unofficial Project Manager*

28. Make High-Value Decisions—*The 5 Choices to Extraordinary Productivity*

29. Lead Through Change—*The 6 Critical Practices for Leading a Team*

30. Get Better—*Get Better: 15 Proven Practices to Building Effective Relationships at Work; The Speed of Trust*

MANAGEMENT MESS TO LEADERSHIP SUCCESS

ACKNOWLEDGMENTS

Almost exactly a year before this book came to life, a team of talented associates at FranklinCovey met to assemble a collection of challenges drawn from across many leadership solutions offered to our clients.

For several weeks, this team, led by my colleague and friend James, met and brainstormed, debated, argued (my favorite part), and eventually settled on thirty leadership challenges, which we used to create a deck of cards. We offered these cards to our certified client facilitators in a campaign intended to build and sustain their leadership skills, and the response was phenomenal: Requests poured in to order additional decks of cards for colleagues, friends, and family members. The interest spurred in me the idea to take the deck a step further and talk candidly about my own leadership journey and its countless potholes.

This original group of very smart people included James (Jimmy) McDermott, Megan Thompson, Matt Murdoch, Leigh Stevens, Sue Dathe-Douglass and Michael Elwell. To each of you, thanks for enthusiastically supporting my efforts to turn your leadership ideas into my own professional therapy.

Bob Whitman, FranklinCovey's Chairman and CEO, helped to curate, winnow, and sequence the list of thirty Challenges. He supports me in all of my endeavors, and he's believed in this book from the beginning. Thanks, Bob, for your continued confidence in me. There's no better professional feeling than knowing your leader has your back. Bob always has my back.

Todd Davis, FranklinCovey's Chief People Officer and my personal Jiminy Cricket, was instrumental in helping select the challenges and edit any overdisclosures. Todd gently reminded me that this book doesn't necessarily replace the confessional—that little room with the screen I'm encouraged to visit periodically as a Catholic. Todd is the very definition of friendship. He's that rare person you meet, who several hundred people think is their best friend. Todd is the real deal. If you've not read his bestselling book, *Get Better: 15 Proven Practices to Building Effective Relationships at Work*, pick it up; it's a beautiful guide to what's most important in life. And

Todd delivers a killer keynote if you're in need of one (and only, of course, if I'm not available).

To my friends at Mango Media, namely the publisher and president Chris McKenney, and my dear friend Michelle Lewy, thank you all for your encouragement and confidence. You both have believed in me from our first encounter, and I promise to remember you when I'm famous—or broke. Also, to Scott McKenney: When we went to lunch at Ortanique, it was you, specifically, who gave me liftoff. I wasn't sure I was going to complete this book, but you emboldened me. When you leaned across the table and insisted I share my leadership stories, that was truly the turning point for me. When a sage tells you to do something, only a fool doesn't. Thank you, Scott.

Thank you, MJ Fievre. MJ's been nicknamed (by me, and for obvious reasons) Miami's "Velvet Hammer." When MJ speaks, everyone around her shuts up and listens. Back in the '80s, MJ, this was known as the E.F. Hutton effect. (You're too young to remember, so Google it.) I've learned from MJ to discern the difference between when smart people talk and when wise people impart. MJ is wise and imparts. And she's kind. The world needs more MJs. What better compliment could someone pay you? But what's with that Disney World fixation? Girl, you gotta find a new hobby!

To Mitchell Kaplan, owner of the iconic literary destination Books and Books in Coral Gables, Florida: Dude, you're legit. You are insanely hard-working and I want to be more like you. I am captivated by so many parts of your life. You're a teacher, coach and mentor, a risk-taking entrepreneur, and a champion of the arts and literature. You're a designer, a curator, and a great husband, father, and friend. But most of all, I am inspired by your unabashed abundance. Your charity, generosity, and belief in others (me) is contagious. Whenever I leave you, I want to be kinder and more helpful to others. Keep spreading your love, Mitchell. You're what Dr. Stephen R. Covey called a servant-leader. It's people like you that my other personal hero, George H. W. Bush, called "a thousand points of light." And to those of you who were confused by that term, Google Mitchell Kaplan. He's what President Bush (41) really meant.

A sincere appreciation to FranklinCovey's thought-leadership team: Annie Oswald, Zach Kristensen, Drew Young, Deb Lund, and Travis

Rust. So many blush-worthy laughs along the journey! Remember, what's said in the room stays in the room. Please.

To our publicist, Ashley Sandberg: I appreciate your friendship and coaching. You're smart and wise. That's the ultimate compliment. And my wife likes you—that's rare. You know everyone, and every one of them adores and respects you. And that's a good thing... (pun intended).

Every significant structure has an architect. They work, unassuming, behind the scenes, crafting stunning beauty that unveils to great acclaim. For renowned works, we know their names well: I. M. Pei, Phillip Johnson, and Daniel Libeskind (although I'm guessing 99 percent of the people who take selfies of themselves at the glass pyramid in front of the Louvre can't tell you who I. M. Pei is, or how he was involved in this masterpiece).

Let's be clear: *Management Mess* ain't no glass pyramid. But it did have an unassuming architect, working behind the scenes, fixing structurally unsound designs, smoothing out rough edges, and teasing out the owner's (that's me) deeper insights and learnings. Platte Clark is my architect. I am grateful to you, Platte, for so much enjoyment, perseverance and, truly, the love you showed me over this journey. You were indispensable in bringing this to life. I am excited to continue working with you on upcoming manuscripts, if you'll have me.

Many friends read my draft manuscripts in varying formats. Some of you, in particular, championed me, and I will never forget your encouragement: Nancy Moore, Pat Lucas, Jennifer Stenlake, Claire Chitwood, Gary Judd, Juliet Dixon, Kim McNally, and Valerie and Barry Boone. Many others made countless notes and suggestions, and to each of you, I am grateful and humbled.

Oh, yeah, a few more—Jon Lofgren, who leads FranklinCovey's social-media strategy and was the original impetus for me to start writing. Thanks, Jon, for the kickstart. And to Chuck Farnsworth, the cowboy who never stopped believing in my potential and continues to be my biggest fan.

My wife suffered (this is not a metaphor) through forced readings and made sure the stories were truthful. She's convinced this book is a career ender for me and I'll never get a real job again. I fear (hope) she's right. Hey, Stephanie, maybe this could be a new gig for us: speaking to unfiltered leaders yearning to make a difference but in need of some guidance. If you're one of those leaders, email me at scott.miller@franklincovey.com. I'd be honored to speak to your team of leadership messes and guide them toward success.

SCOTT

NOTES AND REFERENCES

Part 1: Lead Yourself

P. 18 **Todd Davis quote:** Todd Davis, *Get Better* (New York: Simon & Schuster, 2017).

P. 19 **Stephen R. Covey quote:** Stephen R. Covey, *The 7 Habits of Highly Effective People* (New York: Simon & Schuster, 2013).

P. 30 **Her seminal book claimed the #1 *New York Times* bestseller position for an amazing eight consecutive months:** Deborah Tannen, *You Just Don't Understand* (New York: William Morrow & Co, 1990).

P. 38 **Stephen M. R. Covey quote:** Stephen M. R. Covey and Rebecca R. Merrill, *The Speed of Trust* (New York: Simon & Schuster, 2018).

P. 40 **Blaine Lee quote:** Blaine Lee, *The Power Principle: Influence with Honor* (New York: Simon & Schuster, 1997).

P. 46 **Roger Merrill quote:** Stephen R. Covey, A. Roger Merrill, and Rebecca R. Merrill, *First Things First* (New York: Simon & Schuster, 1994).

P. 66 **24 percent of Americans reported they hadn't taken a vacation in more than a year, and 52 percent reported having unused vacation days at the end of 2017:** "Time Off and Vacation Usage." *U.S. Travel Association*. https://bit.ly/2JOrOrd

Part 2: Lead Others

P. 75 **Jim Collins quote:** Jim Collins, *Good to Great* (New York: Random House Business, 2001).

P. 81 **Stephen R. Covey quote:** Stephen R. Covey, *The 7 Habits of Highly Effective People* (New York: Simon & Schuster, 2013).

P. 103 **Researchers have found that lying to "help" another person is almost always perceived to be good, while lying that had no effect on the other person or that harmed someone is perceived to be wrong:** Business Ethics Research Video North America. "Is Every Lie 'a Sin'? Maybe Not." *Knowledge@Wharton*, September 17, 2014. https://whr.tn/1qLGRBw

P. 104 **Stephen M. R. Covey quote:** Stephen M. R. Covey and Rebecca R. Merrill, *The Speed of Trust* (New York: Simon & Schuster, 2018).

P. 114 **Stephen R. Covey quote:** Stephen R. Covey, *The 7 Habits of Highly Effective People* (New York: Simon & Schuster, 2013).

P. 114 **Stephen M. R. Covey quote:** From 13 Behaviors® of High-Trust Leaders

P. 121 **Absent safety, our old lizard brains ratchet up our sense of risk:** Russell C. Smith and Michael Fister, "Lies, Truth, and Compromises: Are We Hardwired to Lie?" *Psychology Today*, June 15, 2014. https://bit.ly/2uAU06o

P. 126 **Ironically, these feelings often drive an even higher sense of self-worth and personal integrity:** Tyler G. Okimoto, Michael Wenzel, and Kyli Hedrick, "Refusing to Apologize Can Have Psychological Benefits (and We Issue No Mea Culpa for This Research Finding)," *The Canadian Journal of Chemical Engineering*, November 4, 2012. https://bit.ly/2Yy8vpx

P. 132 **Elisabeth Kubler-Ross famously outlined five stages of grief:** Elisabeth Kubler-Ross, *On Death and Dying* (New York: Scribner, 1997).

P. 138 **I wasn't adept at protecting my team against urgencies:** Kory Kogon, Adam Merrill, and Leena Rinne, *The 5 Choices: The Path to Extraordinary Productivity* (New York: Simon & Schuster, 2015).

P. 146 **We dedicate an entire practice to holding effective 1-on-1s:** Scott Miller, Todd Davis, and Victoria Roos-Olsson, *Everyone Deserves a Great Manager: The 6 Critical Practices for Leading a Team* (New York: Simon and Schuster, 2019).

P. 150 **Liz Wiseman invites leaders to assess several key questions:** Liz Wiseman, *Multipliers: How the Best Leaders Make Everyone Smarter* (New York: HarperBusiness, 2017).

Part 3: Get Results

P. 165 **Chris McChesney, Sean Covey, and Jim Huling quote:** Chris McChesney, Sean Covey, and Jim Huling, *The 4 Disciplines of Execution* (New York: Free Press, 2012).

P. 182 **The writer was referencing the 2015 race when Mike Smith pulled up Shared Belief midway through the $1.5 million Charles Town Classic:** Richard Mauntah, "Jockey's Decision Likely Saves Horse from Injury," *Toronto Sun*, April 20, 2015. https://bit.ly/2Yz8rWH

P. 183 **The authors found that 90 percent of managers squandered their time, while only 10 percent of managers spent their time in productive, committed, and reflective ways:** Heike Bruch and Sumantra Ghoshal, "Beware the Busy Manager," *Harvard Business Review*, November 18, 2014. https://bit.ly/2CM9ER3

P. 189 **Erma Bombeck quote:** Erma Bombeck, *Eat Less Cottage Cheese and More Ice Cream: Thoughts on Life from Erma Bombeck* (Kansas City: Andrews McMeel Publishing, 2003).

P. 204 **88 percent of us take on a pessimistic outlook with change**: Alan

Deutschman, *Change or Die: The Three Keys to Change at Work and in Life* (New York: Harper, 2008).

P. 212   **Brené Brown quote:** Brené Brown, *Rising Strong: The Reckoning, The Rumble, The Revolution* (New York: Spiegel & Grau, 2015).

INDEX

SCOTT JEFFREY MILLER

Entering his twenty-third year with FranklinCovey Co., Scott Miller serves as the Executive Vice President of Thought Leadership. He is the host of the FranklinCovey sponsored *On Leadership With Scott Miller*, a weekly leadership webcast, podcast, and newsletter that features interviews with renowned business titans, authors, and thought leaders and is distributed to more than five million business leaders worldwide. He is also the host of the weekly radio program *Great Life, Great Career With Scott Miller* on iHeartMedia's KNRS 105.9. This radio program and podcast provide insight and strategies drawn from FranklinCovey's leadership principles and from Miller's career and personal life experience to assist listeners in becoming more effective as business leaders and to improve their personal performance. Additionally, Miller authors a weekly leadership column for Inc. Magazine.

Miller leads the strategy, development, and publication of FranklinCovey's bestselling books and thought leadership, which provide the framework for the company's world-renowned content and solutions. He is the author of FranklinCovey's *Management Mess to Leadership Success: Become the Leader You Would Follow* (Mango Media). He is also co-authoring *Everyone Deserves A Great Manager: The 6 Critical Practices for Leading a Team*, scheduled to be released in October 2019 (Simon & Schuster)

In his previous roles as Executive Vice President of Business Development and Chief Marketing Officer, Scott led the global transformation of FranklinCovey's brand. Prior to that, as General Manager of Client Facilitation Services, Miller worked with thousands of clients and client facilitators in numerous markets in over thirty countries. He has presented to hundreds of audiences across every industry, and loves to share his unique journey as an unfiltered leader thriving in today's highly-filtered, corporate culture.

Miller joined Covey Leadership Center in 1996 as a client partner with the Education Division, which focused on serving K-12 schools and higher education. He also served as the general manager of FranklinCovey's Central Region for six years in Chicago

Miller began his professional career in 1992 with the Disney Development Company (the real estate development division of Walt Disney Company) as a founding member of the development team that designed the town of Celebration, Florida.

Miller and his wife live in Salt Lake City, Utah, with their three sons.

FranklinCovey
ALL ACCESS PASS

The FranklinCovey All Access Pass provides unlimited access to our best-in-class content and solutions, allowing you to expand your reach, achieve your business objectives, and sustainably impact performance across your organization.

AS A PASSHOLDER, YOU CAN:

- Access FranklinCovey's world-class content, whenever and wherever you need it, including *The 7 Habits of Highly Effective People®: Signature Edition 4.0,* Leading at the *Speed of Trust®,* and *The 5 Choices to Extraordinary Productivity®.*

- Certify your internal facilitators to teach our content, deploy FranklinCovey consultants, or use digital content to reach your learners with the behavior-changing content you require.

- Have access to a certified implementation specialist who will help design impact journeys for behavior change.

- Organize FranklinCovey content around your specific business-related needs.

- Build a common learning experience throughout your entire global organization with our core-content areas, localized into 16 languages.

- Join thousands of organizations using the All Access Pass to implement strategy, close operational gaps, increase sales, drive customer loyalty, and improve employee engagement.

To learn more, visit
FRANKLINCOVEY.COM or call 1-888-868-1776.

FranklinCovey
THE ULTIMATE COMPETITIVE ADVANTAGE

THE ULTIMATE COMPETITIVE ADVANTAGE

FranklinCovey is a global company specializing in organizational performance improvement. We help organizations achieve results that require a change in human behavior.

Our expertise is in seven areas.

LEADERSHIP

Develops highly effective leaders who engage others to achieve results

EXECUTION

Enables organizations to execute strategies that require a change in human beavior.

PRODUCTIVITY

Equips people to make high-value choices and execute with excellence in the mdist of competing priorities.

TRUST

Builds a high-trust culture of collaboration and engagement, resulting in greater speed and lower costs.

SALES PERFORMANCE

Transforms the buyer-seller relationship by helping clients succeed.

CUSTOMER LOYALTY

Drives faster growth and improves frontline performance with accurate customer - and employee-loyalty data.

EDUCATION

Helps schools tranform their performance by unleashing the greatness in every educator and student.

SUBSCRIBE AND LISTEN
TO SCOTT'S WEEKLY RADIO SHOW AND PODCASTS

 FranklinCovey. |  iHeartMEDIA

Great Life, Great Career
HOSTED BY SCOTT MILLER

Great Life, Great Career With Scott Miller brings together insights, proven principles, and expert advice on aligning your passions and talents with your purpose and mission.

 Listen on **Apple Podcasts**  Listen on **Google Podcasts**   LISTEN ON **STITCHER**   Listen On **Spotify**

FRANKLINCOVEY
ONLEADERSHIP
WITH SCOTT MILLER

Join FranklinCovey's executive vice president Scott Miller for weekly interviews with thought leaders, bestselling authors, and world-renowned experts on the topics of organizational culture, leadership development, execution, and personal productivity.

SOME FEATURED INTERVIEWS INCLUDE:

STEPHEN M. R. COVEY
THE SPEED OF TRUST®

KORY KOGON
THE 5 CHOICES®

SUSAN CAIN
THE QUIET REVOLUTION

LIZ WISEMAN
MULTIPLIERS

SETH GODIN
WORK THAT MATTERS FOR
PEOPLE THAT CARE

DR. DANIEL AMEN
CHANGE YOUR BRAIN,
CHANGE YOUR LIFE

Join the ongoing leadership conversation at
FRANKLINCOVEY.COM/ONLEADERSHIP.

SCHEDULE

SCOTT MILLER
TO SPEAK AT YOUR EVENT

Are you planning an event for your organization? Schedule Scott Miller to deliver an engaging keynote speech tailor-made for today's leaders at events including:

- Association and Industry Conferences
- Sales Conferences
- Executive and Board Retreats

- Annual Meetings
- Company Functions
- Onsite Consulting
- Client Engagements

Scott Miller has spoken at hundreds of conferences and client events worldwide and is the host of multiple podcasts and the iHeartRadio show *Great Life, Great Career With Scott Miller*.

To schedule Scott Miller today, call
1-888-554-1776
or visit **franklincovey.com**.

FranklinCovey
THE ULTIMATE COMPETITIVE ADVANTAGE